Organizational Culture, Rule-Governed Behavior and Organizational Behavior Management: Theoretical Foundations and Implications for Research and Practice

Organizational Culture, Rule-Governed Behavior and Organizational Behavior Management: Theoretical Foundations and Implications for Research and Practice

Thomas C. Mawhinney, PhD

Editor

Routledge
Taylor & Francis Group

NEW YORK AND LONDON

First Published by

The Haworth Press, Inc., 10 Alice Street, Binghamton, NY 13904-1580, USA

Transferred to Digital Printing 2011 by Routledge
711 Third Avenue, New York, NY 10017
2 Park Square, Milton Park, Abingdon, Oxon, OX14 4RN

*Organizational Culture, Rule-Governed Behavior and Organizational Behavior Management:
Theoretical Foundations and Implications for Research and Practice* has also been published as
Journal of Organizational Behavior Management, Volume 12, Number 2 1992.

Library of Congress Cataloging-in-Publication Data

Organizational culture, rule-governed behavior and organizational behavior management : theoretical foundations and implications for research and practice / Thomas C. Mawhinney, editor.
     p. cm.
    Includes bibliographical references.
    ISBN 1-56024-359-7
    ISBN 0-78900-068-7 (pbk)
    1. Organizational behavior. 2. Corporate culture. I. Mawhinney, Thomas C.
HD58.7.07364 1992
302.3'5-dc20   92-30026
                                                              CIP

Publisher's Note
The publisher has gone to great lengths to ensure the quality of this reprint
but points out that some imperfections in the original may be apparent.

Organizational Culture, Rule-Governed Behavior and Organizational Behavior Management: Theoretical Foundations and Implications for Research and Practice

CONTENTS

**COMMENTS ON MALOTT'S THEORY PAPER
AND THE THEORETICAL ANALYSIS
BY MALOTT, SHIMAMUNE, AND MALOTT**

A THEORETICAL ANALYSIS OF RULE-GOVERNED BEHAVIOR AND AN OBM INTERVENTION WITHIN STRUCTURAL AND CULTURAL CONSTRAINTS

ABOUT THE EDITOR

Thomas C. Mawhinney, PhD, is Professor of Organizational Behavior and Human Resources Management at the College of Business Administration, University of Detroit Mercy. He has published reviews, conceptual and empirical research articles in the areas of leadership, work motivation (intrinsic-extrinsic reward issues), behavior analyses in work settings, behavior analyses and theories of decision making, and the role of psychological theories in explanation of individual and group responses to productivity improvement programs (e.g., statistical process control and productivity gainsharing). Recently he analyzed the origins of organizational cultural contingencies with an analog to Darwinian evolutionary processes using organizational ecology as a framework for an organizational behavior analysis (OBA). In addition to his publications in the *Journal of Organizational Behavior Management,* Dr. Mawhinney has published articles in *Journal of the Experimental Analysis of Behavior, Journal of Applied Psychology, Organizational Behavior and Human Performance* (now *OB and Human Decision Processes*), *Psychological Reports, Academy of Management Review,* and the *Journal of Management.* His current research concerns behavior analyses of leadership, behavior analytic approaches to judgement, choice, and decision making and their relation with rule governed behavior, behavior analyses of work motivation, behavior analyses of organizational cultural and performance improvement processes from OBA, OBM, and multi-disciplinary vantage points including relationships among, but not limited to, the following: Behavior Analysis, Organizational Behavior Analysis, Organizational Behavior Management, Organizational Behavior, I/O Psychology, Social Psychology, Cultural Anthropology, Human Resources Management, Industrial Relations, and biological analogies in Organizational Theory. Dr. Mawhinney is the editor of the *Journal of Organizational Behavior Management.*

Preface

ANALYSIS OF CULTURE CONCEPTS, RULE-GOVERNED BEHAVIOR AND RELATED PARADOXES

I have had the good fortune of deciding to present new directions for OBM at a time when other members of the field are providing for the review process related materials which dovetail neatly with the new directions I seek to stimulate and to support. The agenda to be supported may appear paradoxical. This is because it suggests a simultaneous emphasis on broadening and narrowing our conceptual focus on organizational behavior processes. In addition, it suggests simultaneously loosening and tightening criteria for admitting data as evidence concerning the processes studied. Finally, it suggests that we keep a unique identity while developing relations with other disciplines.

In the first article in this volume I consider again the problem concerning the degree to which organizational contextual factors contribute to (or detract from) the contributions OBM interventions can make to an organization's overall effectiveness and survival (cf. Mawhinney, 1984). In the current analysis, however, the process I examine operates on organizational populations or across organizational cultures as opposed to within one culture. I present the hypothesis that the elusive origins of social contingencies or so called "organizational cultural variables" are the consequence of a process of selection by consequences. This selection process operates on variations among both newly created cultures and existing organizations composing a population (e.g., members of the steel or auto industry) and selects from among them in Darwinian fashion those which will be extinguished (killed or disbanded). The survivors of the selection process observed during a short span of time are an assortment of organizations engaging in cultural practices which fit each survivor for continued life under current conditions of their shared environment. But the cultural practices are not necessarily practices which will insure survival following a major shift in the environment unless they are practices which focus members' attention on predicting and preparing for such shifts. OBM offers practicing managers an array of rules for constructing contingencies among organizational members' performance-related-behaviors and potentially reinforcing consequences. Some of the rules, such as those related to analyzing organization-wide problems, should be correlated with long term organizational success.

OBM theorists and researchers have identified cultural practices which can contribute to or mitigate the negative effects of job related stress in work environments (Ivancevich & Ganster, 1986). They have related statistical process control to operant behavior processes and individual, group, and organizational performance quality (Mawhinney, 1986; Mawhinney, 1987). They have related cultural practices concerning distribution of organizational rewards among organizational members, members' performance rate and quality, and organizational level performances (Hopkins & Mawhinney, 1992). And, they have considered the issue how to achieve performance excellence from the shop floor level through intermediate levels to the level of the organization as a whole (Redmon & Dickinson, 1990). Although some of the contingencies which foster cultural practices influencing organizational effectiveness are more important than others, potentially every intervention described in JOBM, if implemented on a larger scale, could make an overall difference in whether an organization survived or failed. However, an organization, even when it utilizes all OBM practices known to support superior individual and group performances at the shop floor and middle management levels, can fail in spite of these "good" practices. Failures often occur when chief decision makers improperly align the organization with its environment in terms of important factors such as the following: (1) financial leveraging for profit enhancement, (2) allocating funds to pay dividends in the short term instead of reinvesting in long run development, and (3) entering a line of business or service in which the organization's culture is low on the technological/skill combinations required to succeed. My analysis suggests that organizations still depend critically on the rules followed by chief decision makers at or near the top of organizational hierarchies of authority and responsibility. In short, it suggests we need to know more about rule-governed behavior in general and more importantly how rules are adopted by chief decision makers at the top.

How to deal with the culture concept and understand cultural processes from a behavior analytic vantage point is developed in the second article by Eubanks and Lloyd. Their analysis and mine suggest that our traditional methods of data analysis may need to change. Changes are required to deal with certain group phenomena associated with cultural issues at the level of organizational populations and group processes within organizations.

Important and sometimes pivotal choices made by chief organizational decision makers exemplify a process of rule-governed behavior. The origins of rules followed and the contingencies which determine both choice of rules and the timing of their implementation are clearly important questions for anyone who hopes to understand why some cultural practices in organizations are selected for support by chief decision makers. This process takes place at the individual level within a social context and requires a tightening of conceptual focus and research methods to better understand it. The second section of this issue is devoted to presenting two important ways of conceptualizing rule-governed behavior; the first by Malott and the second by Agnew and Redmon.

Developing useful conceptualizations and research about rule-governed behavior will benefit from an exchange of ideas. In support of this agenda Baer, Baum, and Rachlin provide critical commentary on Malott's theory. There appears to be a divergence of opinion concerning whether a new conceptualization of rule-governed behavior such as Malott's is required. Indeed there appears to be some question whether it is understood by other behavior analysts. If theorists and researchers who share a basic history concerning the analysis of behavior come to divergent perspectives on it, imagine how difficult it will be to communicate with others who do not share common ground in terms of a root paradigm, i.e., behavior analysis. Our discussions about these issues should be aimed at preparing the way for efficient and effective experimental analyses of the phenomenon called rule-governed behavior. There appears to be as much agreement concerning the practical utility of Malott's taxonomy of three OBM contingencies as there is disagreement concerning how rules function to control behavior in the theory per se. For example, my analysis of cultural evolution depends on ineffective indirect acting contingencies and the failure of chief decision makers to somehow make them direct acting with respect to their own strategic management decisions. If every CEO responded to the "real" survival contingencies of the organizational culture being managed, there would be few business failures. In retrospect we are all capable of "seeing" the contingencies which extinguished organizations. An important research agenda is suggested by Malott's taxonomy. It concerns the question whether chief decision makers can be brought under the control of direct acting contingencies which enhance the prospects of their organizations' survival, prosperity of organizational members, and without destruction of natural resources required for survival of the human species, e.g., ozone depletion.

Agnew and Redmon reiterate a point I made in 1975; loose use or incorrect use of terminology can result in loose applications and poor results by practitioners who rely on academic theorists and researchers for leadership in the development of interventions (Mawhinney, 1975). At that time I argued that direct observation of behavior was required to produce data which would permit one to tease out effects of antecedents and consequences on performance-related-behaviors in organizations. Better observational methods are exemplified in observational schemes and research by Komaki and her colleagues (Komaki, 1986; Komaki, Zlotnick, & Jensen, 1986) and by Luthans and his colleagues (Luthans, Rosenkrantz, & Hennessey, 1985). Methods such as the ones they have developed are needed to evaluate rule-following behavior in field settings. Laboratory research need not, however, wait for new methods of data collection. And, we need not wait for new methods to correctly describe the role of rule-governed behavior in interventions aimed at controlling accomplishments or performances. But research which focuses on average performances across group members will not reveal existence of different rules precipitated by a common intervention, e.g., when some people follow a rule supporting the intervention while others follow a rule to resist it (Mawhinney & Gowen, 1990). Only when different groups follow different rules in response to a common intervention will group means be informative about such processes (e.g., Gowen & Jennings, 1990). That is, group mean performance as a summary measure of intervention effectiveness cannot reveal effects of differences among subjects responding individually to different rules whether subjects are taken individually or as work group units (e.g., departments). Thus, in general, field and lab studies of rule-governed behavior need to be more detailed. At the very least they need to reflect an understanding of rule-governed behavior processes. To exemplify how rule-governed behavior occurs in OBM interventions Malott, Shimamune, and Malott provide a step-by-step example in the last section of this issue. The line of reasoning I have presented here suggests that in the future, researchers will need to pay greater attention to the objective(s) of their research and collect and present data congruent with the subject examined. They will need to provide *justification* for methods of data collection and analysis they employ in view of the vantage point they adopt, e.g., rule-governed versus immediate consequence shaped behavior.

Unless an OBM intervention is large scale, i.e., involves the organization from the top down, it must contend with the structural and social context in which it is to occur. Sulzer-Azaroff, Pollack, and Fleming describe an effective OBM intervention which was designed to work within existing structural and cultural constraints. Structural constraints differ depending on whether the setting is a for-profit or a public bureaucratic organization. Sulzer-Azaroff, Pollack, and Fleming took these contextual factors into consideration when developing positive cultural practices with an OBM intervention subject to constraints in the setting. Until OBM is embraced by top, middle, and lower level organizational members at the same time, interventions such as theirs must be fitted into existing conditions. They provide an excellent example of how to analyze the situation to produce results.

Thomas C. Mawhinney
Editor

REFERENCES

Hopkins, B. L., & Mawhinney, T. C. (Eds.). (1992). Pay for performance: History, controversy, and evidence [Special Issue]. *Journal of Organizational Behavior Management, 12*(1).

Gowen, C. R., III, & Jennings, S. A. (1990). The effects of changes in participation and group size on gainsharing success: A case study. *Journal of Organizational Behavior Management, 11*(2), 147-169.

Ivancevich, J. M., & Ganster, D. C. (Eds.). (1986). Job stress: From theory to suggestion [Special Issue]. *Journal of Organizational Behavior Management, 8*(2).

Komaki, J. L. (1986). Toward effective supervision: An operant analysis and comparison of managers at work. *Journal of Applied Psychology, 71*, 270-279.

Komaki, J. L., Zlotnick, S., & Jensen, M. (1986). Development of an operant-based taxonomy and observational index of supervisory behavior. *Journal of Applied Psychology, 71*, 260-269.

Luthans, F., Rosenkrantz, S., & Hennessey, H. W. (1985). What do successful managers really do? An observational study of managerial activities. *Journal of Applied Behavioral Science, 21*, 255-270.

Mawhinney, T. C. (1975). Operant terms and concepts in the description of individual work behavior: Some problems of interpretation, application, and evaluation. *Journal of Applied Psychology, 60*, 704-712.

Mawhinney, T.C. (1984). Philosophical and ethical aspects of organizational behavior management: Some evaluative feedback. *Journal of Organizational Behavior Management, 6*, 5-31.

Mawhinney, T.C. (Ed.). (1987). Organizational behavior management and statistical process control: Theory, technology, and research [Special Issue]. *Journal of Organizational Behavior Management, 9*(1).

Mawhinney, T. C., & Gowen, C. R., III (1990). Gainsharing and the law of effect as the matching law: A theoretical framework. *Journal of Organizational Behavior Management, 11*(2), 61-75.

Redmon, W. K., & Dickinson, A. M. (1990). Promoting excellence through performance management [Special Issue]. *Journal of Organizational Behavior Management, 11*(1).

ANALYSIS OF CULTURAL PROCESSES AND CONCEPTS: MACRO AND MICRO LEVELS

Evolution of Organizational Cultures as Selection by Consequences: The Gaia Hypothesis, Metacontingencies, and Organizational Ecology

T. C. Mawhinney

SUMMARY. Terms, concepts, and theories from biology, cultural anthropology, and behavior analysis are integrated to explain the evolution of organizational cultural practices. The universal concept in all three disciplines is natural selection by consequences as a causal mode which accounts for behavior of individuals, groups of

T. C. Mawhinney is affiliated with the University of Detroit Mercy.

Address correspondence to: T. C. Mawhinney, College of Business, University of Detroit Mercy, 4001 W. McNichols Road, Detroit, MI 48221.

Portions of this article were presented in a paper entitled "Positive and negative corporate culture: Two exemplars" in a symposium entitled *Rule-Governed Behavior, Organizational Cultures and OBM* presented at the 1990 annual Association for Behavior Analysis (an international organization) meetings, Nashville, TN, May 29, 1990.

Helpful editorial comments and reactions to an earlier draft of the paper were provided by Sigrid S. Glenn and Richard W. Malott.

people, and births and deaths of entire organizational cultures. These selection processes provide a theoretical framework which suggests a multi-disciplinary research agenda.

Selection as a causal mode in the evolution of behavioral processes and their relation to cultural evolution are summarized by Skinner (1981) as follows:

> Selection by consequences is a causal mode found only in living things, or machines made by living things. It was first recognized in natural selection, but also accounts for the shaping and mainte-nance of the behavior of the individual and the evolution of cul-tures. In all three of these fields, it replaces explanations based on the causal modes of classical mechanics. The replacement is strong-ly resisted. Natural selection has now made its case, but similar delays in recognizing the role of selection in other fields could deprive us of valuable help in solving the problems which confront us. (Skinner, 1981, p. 501)

Major upheavals in industrial cultures have many undesirable conse-quences for people subjected to them. The collapse of the U.S. Steel Corporation's oligopoly (Adams, 1986) provides a dramatic example, on a larger scale, of a scenario played out year in and year out on a smaller scale among numerous small companies founded only to die soon after. But, the past appears not to function as a prologue for prevention of cultural collapses such as in "big steel." Other industries exhibit similar cultural tendencies which may dispose them to a similar fate.

These problems, huge organizational cultures becoming unstable and collapsing, appear to be related to a "natural process" of industrial cul-tural evolution in which cultures are founded and disband (Hannan & Freeman, 1989). Although the consequences of such processes produce aversive and unavoidable events in the lives of many people who play no direct role in their occurrence, the process has no conscience. The pro-cess is a natural evolutionary one. And, evolutionary processes are amor-al (Gould, 1983).

The natural process of cultural evolution might be forestalled if orga-nizations were more than "machine like" creations of people. Except for mechanical technologies employed in them, organizational cultures are not "machine like" creations of people. Rather, they are complex inter-locking relationships among people in human cultures (Harris, 1979; Glenn, 1988, 1991); *they are living systems* (Miller, 1978). As living systems their behavior is accounted for by a causal mode of selection by consequences. Thus, the position which opposes the applicability of machine metaphors to characterize organizational behavior is well founded while the position which opposes the applicability of biological metaphors is not well founded (cf. Daft & Weick, 1984). Organizations are living systems composed, first, of organized human social behavior and, second, various physical artifacts produced by human behavior.

The idea that displacements associated with organizational deaths can be avoided by invoking rational decision rules and following them is attractive (March & Simon, 1958; Thompson, 1967). After all, decisions made and acted upon at the individual and group levels in organizations eventually translate into the aggregate measures of organizational success and failure at the organizational level of analysis, e.g., profits and losses. Whether individuals or organizations can maximize with respect to a long term objective, such as survival, is problematic. Classical theories of outcome maximization require the decision maker to identify all possible alternative courses of action and the consequences which will accrue to any chosen alternative. Therefore, such theories assume the decision maker has near perfect information regarding current and future states of the decision environment. Within complex organizational choice situations, it is virtually impossible for a decision maker to satisfy this assumption (March & Simon, 1958). On the other hand, in a simple laboratory situation a subject has been able to identify and follow rules of income maximization within a nontrivial choice setting (Mawhinney, 1982). In this experiment the subject, provided with repeated exposures to the set of choices, generated and followed income maximizing rules in what was clearly an instance of learning and problem solving (Skinner, 1968).

When human subjects in choice experiments do not engage in problem solving behavior aimed at maximizing income from repeated choices across time, they do not make optimal choices, and they do depart from optimal choice patterns in ways predicted by melioration and reinforcement matching (Herrnstein, 1990). Optimization or maximization by humans depends on collecting accurate information about how their environment works (i.e., choice-outcome rules or contingencies) and on following optimization or maximization rules when making choices based on the information collected. Incomplete information can limit the decision maker to close approximations rather than ultimate optimization and maximization. Optimization and maximization can also be limited by the individual decision maker's experience with applying normative decision rules. Humans are known to exhibit decision making biases which inhibit optimization and maximization. Normative rules for both information gathering and choice making which prevent known biases are often taught to business school students in organizational behavior courses (see Organ & Bateman, 1991).

Not every top level decision maker has necessarily been exposed to such courses. Even among those who have, application of what has been learned depends upon local cultural contingencies. For example, the organization may or may not have developed the means to provide required information and may or may not reward decision makers for following decision making rules. Thus, avoiding the displacements associated with organizational decline and death is more likely to accrue to organizations which can retain resourceful information concerning how their environments work and provide rewards for decision makers who engage in following normative rules. This is more likely to occur in organizations which can function as interpretive or learning systems that "know" the requirements for survival in the organizations' environments (Daft & Weick, 1984; Hedberg, 1981). In the absence of the support that such organizational systems provide, individuals respond in the present to a future about which their own experiences permit a limited view (Rachlin, 1989). At best, future oriented rule governed choices are attempts to "beat the odds" about what future conditions will come to pass and what organizational responses are most appropriate to make under those conditions.

Many organizational decisions are distributed across time. If the organization survives long enough, decisions are distributed across generations of decision makers and decision making groups. In organizations which are long lived, there exists the opportunity for interpretive and learning systems to evolve within them, whether or not they do evolve. In such cases it is possible for decisions at one point in time to commit the organization to a path from which it is difficult to turn in another direction. This would be particularly true if the interpretive and learning system developed an incorrect vision of requirements for long term survival, while efficiently producing short term benefits. Short run successes might falsely suggest the interpretive system was valid even though short term successes would be at the expense of long term death. Ideally, organizational decision makers would learn to construct and follow rules which integrate costs and benefits which accrue in both short and long term time horizons. For example, long term survival often requires that current profits be forsaken to invest in technological change or updating which will raise the probability of long term survival. Profits and losses occur at the organizational level of analysis even though the decisions upon which they depend occur at the level of the individual(s) or group(s) making critical decisions related to profits and losses. Thus, whenever reference is made to organizational level behavior, e.g., its profitability, flexibility, etc., this behavior is understood to be a summary measure of collective organizational member behavior.

The blame for a dramatic decline of an industry or organization may seem to be the responsibility of its current chief decision maker, group, or system. In reality the decline is often the realization of a process begun at some earlier point in the evolution of the organizational culture. For example, responsibility for collapse of U.S Steel Corporation is not to be found in some single top level decision taken during the crisis of the 1960s and 1970s. The collapse was the consequence of a series of strategic decisions made as early as the organization's founding, just after the turn of the century, and failure of its leadership to invest in and adopt advanced technological innovations on several important occasions. As every top level executive decision then and now, these past decisions were based on an analysis of social contingencies that explain the immediate behavior of top level decision makers and decision making groups (Skinner, 1969). Explaining immediate behavior in terms of social contingencies *is not difficult*. The board of directors may demand a resignation from the executive who fails to deliver dividends to shareholders in the short term. However, explaining the "origins of social contingencies" governing the decision *is* difficult (Skinner, 1953). To understand the origins is to understand the processes governing the evolution of cultural practices in organizations, some of the most important of which shape top level decision making about corporate policies, strategies, and tactics (Gilbert, 1978).

Some organizations appear to defy the odds against them by evolving with their changing environments in the face of changing leadership at the top and wide swings in the business cycle (Handlin, 1992). Should these currently successful organizational cultures serve as models to guide construction of other organizations engaged in producing other goods and services? This approach to building effective organizational cultures would obviate the need to engage in a program of research concerning how cultural evolutionary processes work on formal organizations. But, lessons from history teach that rules extracted from one set of circumstances applied to different circumstances under the assumption that they "should work" everywhere, will, sooner or later, produce unanticipated negative results. For example, reinforcement schedules and other pay systems have actually reduced performance levels in some circumstances (Mawhinney, 1975; Peach & Wren, 1992) and organizations have run up incentive systems expenses while failing to achieve the cost savings to fund them (Redmon & Agnew, 1991). A well developed science regarding the causal processes responsible for a phenomenon (Moxley, 1989; Othersen & Othersen, 1987) (e.g., organizational cultures, organizational effectiveness, and survival) is an important requirement for achieving artfully crafted and effective applications (Cohen & Filipczak, 1989; Zemke & Gunkler, 1982). Thus, before one can effectively deal with issues concerning when and how to intervene in an organizational culture, it is imperative that one understand the historical causes of its current configuration. These causes are found in the *processes* of cultural evolution which have shaped the organizational culture.

The purpose of this article is to introduce two related vantage points on the explanation of organizational cultural evolution. The first is the Gaia Hypothesis which describes all life on earth as the result of a self-organizing and self-regulating ecological system (Lovelock, 1988). The second is an extension of the Gaia Hypothesis applied to the self-organizing and self-regulating behaviors among formal organizations that populate some bounded social/economic environment (Hannan & Freeman, 1989). These two vantage points–evolution of life on earth and evolution of formal organizational populations–correlate with the notions about selection as a causal mode summarized by Skinner (1981) above, i.e., only those life or organizational cultural forms which are maintained by the current environmental consequences of their actions live while others perish. The bridge between the two vantage points and organizational behavior analysis is provided by Glenn's interpretation and extension of Harris' model (1979) called "cultural materialism" in the field of cultural anthropology (Glenn, 1988; 1991).

THE GAIA HYPOTHESIS: EARTH AS A LIVING SYSTEM

Lovelock has taken seriously the possibility that the planet Earth, viewed in its entirety, *is* alive. He named the living planet Gaia (pronounced gay-ah), a name the Greeks gave to the Earth Goddess. He called his hypothesis that Earth lives, the Gaia Hypothesis. He admits, "The idea that the Earth is alive is at the outer bounds of scientific credibility" (Lovelock, 1988, p. 3). Having said that, however, he advances his case using selection by consequences as a causal mode to explain the evolution of all life on Earth. His contention is that all life in the current system shares in the maintenance of atmospheric (and oceanic) parameters required for all current life on the planet and in its seas.

Not accepting teleological explanations, natural scientists prefer objectivity in explanations of the behavior of living systems. Therefore, other scientists initially objected to the Gaia Hypothesis on grounds that it was teleological and seemed to require foresight and planning by the biota; "How in the world could the bacteria, the trees, and the animals have a conference to decide the optimum conditions [for the survival and maintenance of life among all of them]?" (Lovelock, 1988, p. 33). Looking ahead to organizational cultural life, one might well ask the following: How does any one person or group in an organization as complex as GM or the Federal Government plan for and achieve optimal, even minimal conditions for organizational or national life?

Of tremendous intuitive appeal is the idea that "adaptation" accounts for the way things are–that living things and organizations are adapted to local environmental constraints. Individuals see and experience in a relatively constant way the slowly changing contingencies to which they think they can adapt. However, variations in life per se and organizational cultural evolution in particular, change the constraints to which a current life or organizational form may be required to adapt. When the limits of adaptation are exceeded by a changing set of environmental constraints, those life and organizational forms that cannot adapt will perish. At the moment of current observation those forms still in the game of life will appear to have adapted to the current conditions whether or not a process of adaptation or natural selection more accurately accounts for their presence in the current population of living things. All of which is to say, life and evolution are *dynamic*. Lovelock (1988) provides the following characterization:

> Evidence . . . shows the Earth's crust, oceans, and air to be either directly the product of living things or else massively modified by their presence. Consider how the oxygen and nitrogen of the air come directly from plants and microorganisms, and how the chalk and the limestone rocks are the shells of living things once floating in the sea. Life has not adapted to an inert world determined by the dead hand of chemistry and physics. We live in a world that has been built by our ancestors, ancient and modern, and which is continuously maintained by all things alive today. Organisms are adapting in a world whose material state is determined by the activities of their neighbors; this means that changing the environment is part of the game. To think otherwise would require that evolution was a game like cricket or baseball–one in which the rules forbad environmental change. If, in the real world, the activity of an or-

ganism changes its material environment to a more favorable state, and as a consequence it leaves more progeny, then both the species and the change will increase until a new stable state is reached. On a local scale adaptation is a means by which organisms can come to terms with unfavorable environments, but on a planetary scale the coupling between life and its environment is so tight that the tautologous notion of "adaptation" is squeezed from existence. The evolution of the rocks and the air and the evolution of the biota are not to be separated. (Lovelock, 1988, pp. 33-34)

Because current living things remain in the evolutionary game, Gaia is an excellent environment for most life today. But, if a species' neighbors change the environment in ways favorable to them and not to the species, the species' survival can be threatened or the species can be extinguished in one of several ways. In one scenario the species compete for space but not food and the neighbor's population growth rate increases density in the space; the species may be squeezed from its territory, assuming it cannot drive out or kill off its neighbor. In another scenario the two populations compete for a common food source and the neighbor's population growth rate reduces the food supply of the species, again assuming that the species cannot drive out or kill off its neighbor. Less direct is the case in which a neighbor's growth in numbers or methods of interacting with the environment changes the parameters of a more pervasive feature of the environment, e.g., composition of the air and seas on a regional or global scale. Such change may result in extinction of the species while not adversely affecting the neighbor.

Lovelock's partly theoretical and partly factual account of Gaia's history includes evolutionary eras when the human species could not have lived in the atmosphere created by Gaian social life of that time. This is because the balance of oxygen and other gases composing the atmosphere eons ago was not within the parameters which sustain human life. It can be said with confidence, however, that the life which has survived to this point in time (and it need not necessarily survive beyond this time when it is currently on the brink of extinction) is well suited to the current arrangement with neighbors in the sense that they jointly maintain an atmosphere which supports them all. As the recent reports on ozone depletion suggest, however, the condition of the common atmosphere may be changing as a consequence of modern human cultural practices.

A parallel with the evolution of Gaia can be seen in the evolution of the auto industry. The economic, social, and technological environment of the auto industry at the turn of the century would not support the cultural life of today's GM, Ford, or Chrysler. The GM, Ford, and Chrysler cultures which shared their ecosystem with twenty-three other neighbors during the 1920s, whether intended or not, were part of an evolutionary process which extinguished these neighboring auto cultures. Departure of their neighbors improved the economic atmosphere of the Big Three; for a time at least, their adaptation was excellent. Now they have uninvited neighbors from Japan. These neighbors have imported with them some very different cultures. The effects of the new neighbors is evident in the economic atmospheric parameters of the Big Three measured by recent changes in their market shares. As revealed later in this study, the Auto industry's evolutionary history is an example of organizational cultural evolution and adaptation that resembles the evolution of Gaia, a dynamic ecological process within which organizational cultures and environments evolve together.

In order to further comprehend the "organizational ecology" vantage point, it is necessary to briefly sketch the method Lovelock employed to demonstrate plausibility of the Gaia Hypothesis. To demonstrate how two amoral organisms could survive by creating together environmental conditions which neither could produce alone, Lovelock (1988) created a numerical simulation model called Daisyworld. In this model a set of organisms (quantitative models of two servomechanisms) sharing a common environment, without benefit of any related thought processes, acted to regulate the conditions essential to their mutual survival. In the simplest Daisyworld two shades of daisies, light and dark, populated the world model and their relative population size depended on effects of the light:dark daisy population ratio on the atmospheric temperature. Atmospheric temperature was regulated by the degree to which the two populations either reflected the solar radiation (a cooling effect) or absorbed it (a warming effect). If they were to regulate their common requirement for a stable atmospheric temperature, the relative size of the two daisy populations (light and dark) would have to change as a function of incoming solar radiation. Solar luminosity was varied and the Daisyworld model exhibited a strong regulation of planetary temperature across changes in solar luminosity as a consequence of the "simple competitive growth of plants with dark and light shades" (Lovelock, 1988, p. 39). In this way Lovelock disposed of the argument that the members of Gaian society would be required to plan their interactions to achieve their common requirements for a life sustaining ecosystem. Rather than depending on a central decision maker to supply goals to direct behavior within and between the two populations in his causal explanation, he provided another example of selection by consequences as a causal mode within a simulation model of a living system.

To draw an analogy between the regulation of Lovelock's ecological system and the operational system of relatively free competitive economic markets is comprehensible. When applying Lovelock's explanation one can then understand the government's intrusion into industrial economic matters (Greer, 1984) as an attempt to inject human moral responsibility or objectives into an evolutionary process which is intrinsically amoral (Gould, 1983). The rise and fall of "big steel" also provides anecdotal evidence in support of the validity of such an analogy.

METACONTINGENCIES:
THE CULTURAL ANTHROPOLOGY BRIDGE

Two different sources of variation can be identified upon which selection processes may operate: variation arising within one culture and variation arising among different cultures. All variations spring from the behavior of people within one social context or another. The first process, variations within a culture, is captured by a behavior analytic interpretation of terms and concepts from a theory in cultural anthropology called "cultural materialism." It functions to bridge the gap between the scope of selection by consequences as a causal mode governing Gaia and selection of cultural adaptations within and among organizational cultures (i.e., organizational ecology).

Malagodi (1986) suggested behavior analysts adopt the anthropological vantage point Harris (1979) calls "cultural materialism" and consider developing relations with other academic disciplines to direct behavior analyses toward research questions which could benefit from its vantage point. Of particular interest to Malagodi (1986) were social contingencies responsible for decisions made by corporate Chief Executive Officers (CEOs) when selecting corporate goals, objectives, policies, strategies, and tactics. In response, Glenn related Harris' conceptual framework and concepts to behavior analysis (Glenn, 1988) and large scale societal issues arising from cultural practices (Glenn, 1991). Glenn presented the following explanation of cultural practices and the selection process governing their evolution:

> If 2 . . . *n* people repeatedly reenact a particular scene [behavioral episode (Skinner, 1953)] because the behavior of each has become integrated into a repeated pattern through the reinforcement contin-

gencies provided by others, the entire integrated set of contingencies constitutes an instance of a cultural practice. What accounts for the origin of such a unit, its extended survival or its disappearance (lack of behavioral descendants), or its evolution? Variation and selection. As usual, the variation is endogenous (although it [variation or innovation] may be selected as a characteristic), and selection is exogenous. In the case of cultural practices, the selection agent is the outcome (aggregate effects) produced by the practice (interlocking behavioral contingencies). The variation is provided by permutations in the behavior of individuals participating in the practice. (Glenn, 1991, p. 63)

Organizations are composed of diverse interlocking behavioral contingencies resulting from division of labor, specialization of tasks and related skill requirements, and a hierarchy of authority and responsibility for administering rewards and sanctions required to achieve coordination among members' task performances (Mizruchi, 1983; Sulzer-Azaroff, Pollack, & Fleming, 1992). Top-level decision makers are officially sanctioned to select, among variations in cultural practices, those which will receive support by the official organizational culture and those which it will extinguish by using various formal and political reward and penalty systems (Kerr & Slocum, 1981; Melcher, 1976). For example, performance incentive systems and productivity gainsharing systems are sometimes implemented in an effort to increase performance output and reduce per unit production costs (Peach & Wren, 1992). But, in some cases, anticipated effects do not materialize because informal cultural practices provide immediate social reinforcement or punishment for following output restriction rules (Mawhinney & Gowen, 1989). The consequences of performance restrictions are immediate positive social praise (approbation) for workers and may, or may not, have longer-term negative consequences for the total organizational culture. If resistance to industrial cultural control of workers pervades all competitors in an industry (Jermier, 1988), then no one organization enjoys a cost advantage by avoiding the costly practice within its culture (Adams, 1986).

On the other hand, top level decision makers sometimes find it hard to follow a rule (Malott, 1992) which involves a long delayed and improbable aversive consequence, such as the following: Failure to invest in new plant and equipment or adopt new technologies today *might* result in lost industry dominance in twenty, thirty or forty years as higher prices attract competitors to attack your markets (Adams, 1986). Top-level decision makers can and do select from among variations in cultural practices (Lincoln, 1946). They may try to implement practices by imitating useful practices from other existing cultures or by deriving guidelines from academic and research texts about effective organizational designs (Davis & Lawrence, 1977; Nystrom & Starbuck, 1981a; Nystrom & Starbuck, 1981b; Thompson, 1967). But, their primary responsibility is to control critical outcomes of all cultural practices, whether formally or informally supported, within their organization. These global relations are called "metacontingencies."

"Metacontingencies are contingent relations between cultural practices and outcomes of those practices" (Glenn, 1991, p. 62). Top-level organizational decision makers attend to important decisions guided by critical "metacontingencies"; these are complex, dynamic, organizational feedback functions, some of which can be quantified (Baum, 1989). In for-profit organizations the critical organizational measure of ultimate survival is the difference between costs of all operations and revenues from all sources. Variations in profits and losses are determined by complex relationships among organizational cultural practices, including those practices by top-level decision makers themselves, as well as the consequences of cultural practices by other organizational cultures that populate the competitive environment within which an organization operates. For example, cutting costs and prices to compete with other cultures in the population may permit the organization to engage in price competition. However, when all organizations within a population (e.g., U.S. auto industry oligopoly of the 1950s and 1960s) negotiate relatively similar agreements on wages, hours, and conditions of work among unions representing workers across organizations within the organizational population, organizations in that population will exhibit relatively similar labor cost structures (Adams, 1986). Thus, some historical cultural events may function to reduce the flexibility of organizational cultural adaptation by variations from within the existing culture. More importantly, the examples above serve to indicate that metacontingencies related to organizational survival cannot be fully evaluated and may not even be discriminable from the vantage point of an organizational cultural member looking out on the competitive population from within an organizational culture.

Interestingly, Daft and Weick (1984) contend that organizational cultures function as interpretive systems and there exists a typology of interpretive systems among organizations which *do survive*. However, their vantage point *does not* account for how these interpretive systems arose in the first place. Therefore, a logical conclusion of their interpretive systems in conjunction with research results guided by the organizational ecology vantage point (Hannan & Freeman, 1989) is that some organizations have failed to produce within themselves or to imitate other's interpretive systems required for survival. These organizations, of course, are not among the survivors.

CHANGING VANTAGE POINTS: FROM INTRA-ORGANIZATIONAL TO POPULATION DYNAMICS

Entire organizations are born and die as their environments evolve through time and their metacontingencies change. Consider that the number of auto companies reached a peak of 33 between 1900 and 1910, decreased each decade until 1940 and for two decades remained at 9 in number, fell each decade from 1960 to the present Big Three (Figures 1 and 2). It is on this churning population of cultures and their related metacontingencies that a process of selection by consequences has operated on individual organizational cultures. For this reason a population rather than an intraorganizational vantage point is required to "see" and understand the origins of surviving industrial cultures. Organizational births provide cultural variations upon which selection by consequences operates at the level of organizational populations by selecting individual cultures.

> Life is social. It exists in communities and collectives. There is a useful word in physics to describe the properties of collections: *colligative*. It is needed because there is no way to express or measure the temperature or pressure of a single molecule. Temperature and pressure, say the physicists, are colligative properties of a sensible collection of molecules. All collections of living things show properties unexpected from a knowledge of a single one of them. (Lovelock, 1988, p. 18)

Organizational ecology is concerned with learning how "social conditions affect the rates at which new organizations and new organizational forms arise, the rates at which organizations change forms, and the rates at which organizations and forms die out" as well as "the dynamics that take place *within* organizational populations" (Hannan & Freeman, 1989, p. 7). Rates of organizational births, organizational deaths, and degrees of intrapopulation and interpopulation competition are colligative properties of organizations. Although organizational health is a useful construct,

FIGURE 1. Evolution of the U.S. auto industry through ten decades: 1890-1990. Line graphs link population sizes (number of producers), producer births, and mergers across ten decades. Data are plotted for status of the industry during the last year of each decade.

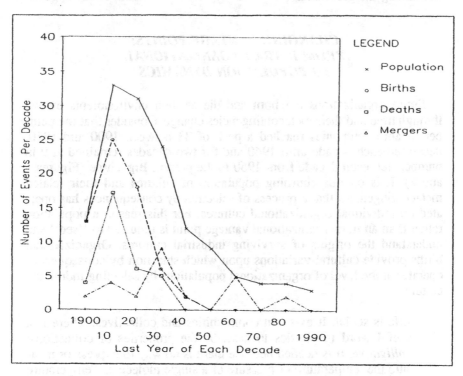

and perhaps an essential construct in organizational behavior analysis (Redmon & Agnew, 1991), within a population an organization cannot have a rate of birth or death. These rates are colligative properties of the population over some interval of time. The birth or death of an organization may involve some time, but each is ultimately binary–organizations are not partly alive or dead–they are either living or dead.

Organizational metacontingencies come into existence when organizations are born. They cease to exist when the organizational culture dies. Living organizations have measurable metacontingencies which integrate effects of internal cultural practices and the practices of other cultures within a given population. When organizational leaders attempt to respond to lost market shares and the cultural practices associated with the

FIGURE 2. Evolution of the U. S. auto industry through ten decades: 1890-1990. Source: Adapted from Adams (1986, p. 128).

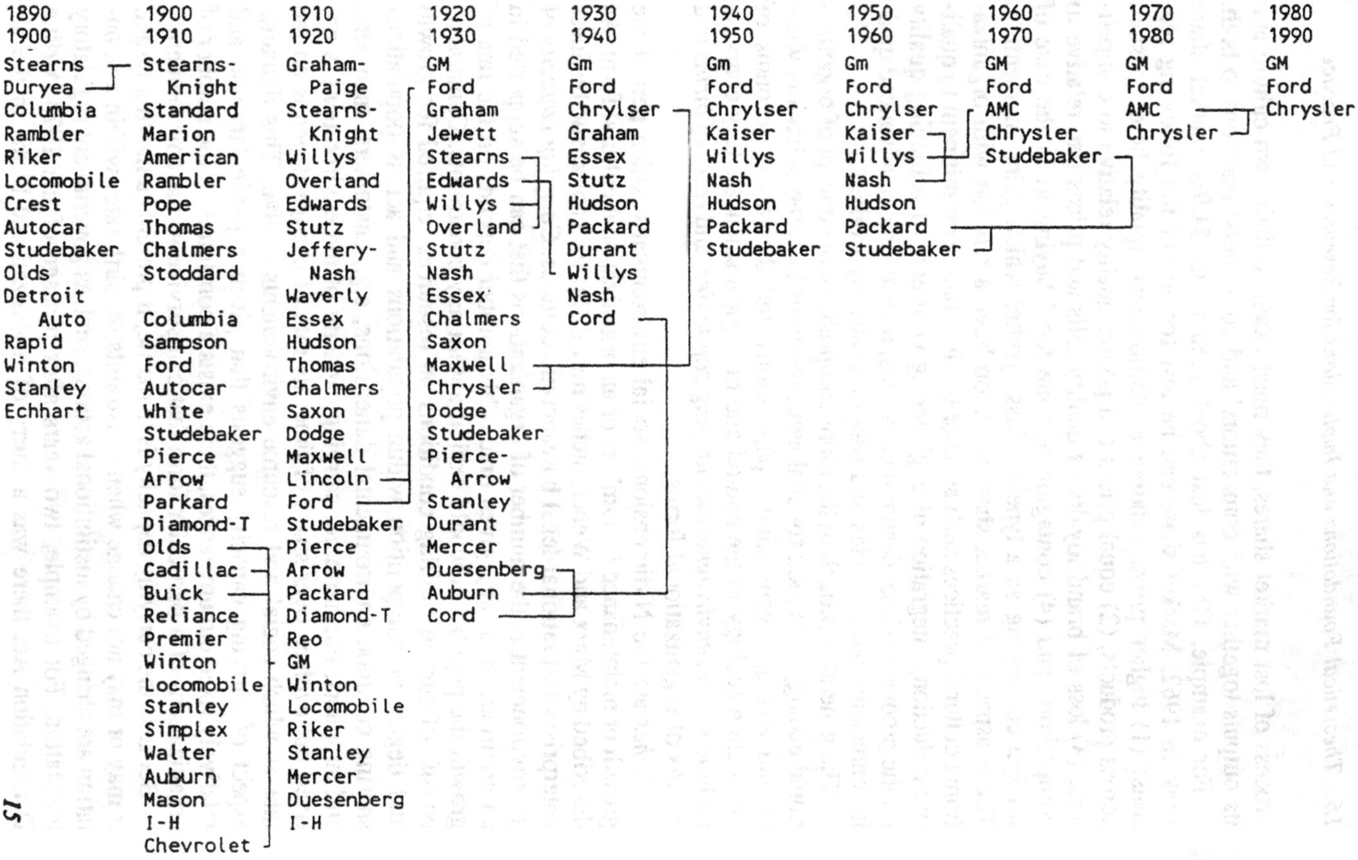

1890 1900
Stearns
Duryea
Columbia
Rambler
Riker
Locomobile
Crest
Autocar
Studebaker
Olds
Detroit Auto
Rapid
Winton
Stanley
Echhart
1900 1910
Stearns-Knight
Standard
Marion
American
Rambler
Pope
Thomas
Chalmers
Stoddard
Columbia
Sampson
Ford
Autocar
White
Studebaker
Pierce Arrow
Parkard
Diamond-T
Olds
Cadillac
Buick
Reliance
Premier
Winton
Locomobile
Stanley
Simplex
Walter
Auburn
Mason
I-H
Chevrolet
1910 1920
Graham-Paige
Stearns-Knight
Willys
Overland
Edwards
Stutz
Jeffery-Nash
Waverly
Essex
Hudson
Thomas
Chalmers
Saxon
Dodge
Maxwell
Lincoln
Ford
Studebaker
Pierce
Arrow
Packard
Diamond-T
Reo
GM
Winton
Locomobile
Riker
Stanley
Mercer
Duesenberg
I-H
1920 1930
GM
Ford
Graham
Jewett
Stearns
Edwards
Willys
Overland
Stutz
Nash
Essex
Chalmers
Saxon
Maxwell
Chrysler
Dodge
Studebaker
Pierce-Arrow
Stanley
Durant
Mercer
Duesenberg
Auburn
Cord
1930 1940
Gm
Ford
Chrylser
Graham
Essex
Stutz
Hudson
Packard
Durant
Willys
Nash
Cord
1940 1950
Gm
Ford
Chrylser
Kaiser
Willys
Nash
Hudson
Packard
Studebaker
1950 1960
Gm
Ford
Chrylser
Kaiser
Willys
Nash
Hudson
Packard
Studebaker
1960 1970
GM
Ford
AMC
Chrysler
Studebaker
1970 1980
GM
Ford
AMC
Chrysler
1980 1990
GM
Ford
Chrysler

process of lost market shares, they must examine their own culture and its outputs together with competitors' and consumers' reactions to both.

For example, GM has lost about 17% of its 51.9% market share peak in 1962. Market share can be lost for any of the following reasons: (1) higher prices relative to competitors, quality held constant across products, (2) equal prices and poorer quality relative to competitors, (3) loss of brand loyalty as quality falls and prices rise relative to competitors, and (4) contagion or "me too" buying as in the case of foreign car buying as a type of class symbol which gains momentum. These aspects of market share variation have a relation with organizational cultural practices such as labor pricing, labor commitment to quality production, integration of engineering with ease of achieving quality on the production line, design innovations, investments in advanced quality enhancing technologies and adoption rates by workers.

The general approach in the more comprehensive concept of organizational ecology is to look for analogous relations between behaviors within and among organizational populations and theoretical accounts of population ecology in the natural and biological sciences. Key concepts include *niches, environmental carrying capacities,* and *rates of births* and *deaths* of organizational forms.

Niches are the N-dimensional social environments which permit the growth or maintenance in numbers of an organizational cultural form. As described by Marx and Weber, niches may differ for capitalistic business enterprises and rational-legal bureaucratic cultures. *Carrying capacity* of an environment is the number of organizations that can be supported in an environment at any given time. This number depends on the rate of growth the population would exhibit absent any constraints. Constraints consist of current limiting conditions on resources required for growth and degree of competition within populations and across populations sharing common environmental dimensions, e.g., customers, members, and suppliers. Furthermore, carrying capacity of the environment is not fixed but evolves over spans of time; its rate of change depends on the rate at which social and resource environments evolve. This dynamic aspect of carrying capacity suggests that given a particular time and relatively fixed circumstances, there exists a constraint on the number of organizations of a particular form that can survive in the environment.

Because the carrying capacity is dynamic, it presents a moving target. It may or may not change when constraints on birth rates within a population are changed by institutional actions, such as government regulatory legislation. For example, two years after passage of the 1978 Airline Deregulation Act there was a flurry of organizational births in the air transportation industry. However, by November 1991 Midway airlines terminated services and the only remaining airline founded after deregulation is in Chapter 11 bankruptcy. These events support the contention by Hannan and Freeman (1989) that carrying capacity of an organizational population environment may not be easily estimated by new entrants into the population. When this is the case, even well conceived organizational cultures have statistically poor odds of survival. This fundamental concept by organizational ecologists is also supported by what organizational behavior analysts can deduce about organizational cultural practices and their origins.

> As in biological and behavioral evolution, cultural evolution has occurred as a result of processes that operate without respect to any future. Cultural practices that exist do so because they fit the environment of a previous time, which is to say that they may not continue to exist [beyond the present]. (Glenn, 1991, p. 65)

Organizational cultural practices well suited for organizational life in an organizational ecology with a gap between size of the existing organizational population and carrying capacity of the environment may not support organizational life when the carrying capacity is approached or exceeded.

Organizational ecologists assume that once some number of organizations are founded within a population, members of the cohort of organizational cultures will vary in the rate at which each adapts to requirements for survival. Rate of adaptive change on the part of the existing cohort depends on their own rates of change which, in turn, change the competitive environment. For example, one organization may set a pace of change which others must match to survive. Or, the pace of adaptive change may be set by births of new organizations which embody the most advanced cultural and technological innovations available for producing goods or services within the population's competitive environment. Whether the pace of change is set by an existing organization or by creation of new organizations, survival of existing organizations depends on their ability to *synchronize* rates of adaptive organizational change with rates of environmental change.

Quite often, however, organizations exhibit cultural and technological inertia which inhibits synchronization of organizational and environmental change. An organization may exhibit constant change in cultural practices and technologies and still fail to survive for two reasons. First, when the organizations' rates of change lag the rate of competitive environmental evolution, they will be exposed to the risk of extinction and, consequently, some will be disbanded. Some organizations will be disbanded because they attempt to change at a rate in excess of what the evolving competitive environment will support. Second, organizations may change at a rate synchronized with rate of change in the competitive environment but are maladaptive with respect to the characteristics of the changes. Replacing disbanded organizations will be new organizations founded with more or, perhaps, all of the most current cultural practices and technologies in place. Unless the newer forms correlate the pace of their *adaptive* change in cultural practices, structural arrangements, and technological innovations with the pace of change in their competitive environment, they will eventually suffer the fate of the organizations they displaced; they too will disband (Hannan and Freeman, 1989).

Organizations in a competitive environment are favored by a rising carrying capacity. But younger ones and older ones with outmoded cultural practices and technologies are more subject to selective pressures (risks of extinction) as the carrying capacity is reached or overshot, whenever this may occur. The selection process according to organizational ecologists is one in which currently better fitted organizational cultures replace those less fitted for the extant evolved state of the competitive environment. Certain evolving entities have failed to remain in the evolutionary game (Skinner, 1981).

The organizational ecology theorists, concerned about the same underlying processes as organizational behavior analysts, profess that the phenomenon of organizational cultural evolution is a social process with colligative properties which are not directly observable; they may not be discriminable among top-level decision makers on the inside of an organization looking out upon its competitive environment. In addition, even if the requirement of organizational cultural change is discriminated by a top-level organizational decision maker, the momentum or cultural inertia within the organization may mitigate against changes in existing cultural practices. Recognition of the requirement for change by someone in an organization will not necessarily cause a change. And, an amoral selection process will extinguish the existing practices if the competitive environment does not support the metacontingencies of which they are a part.

The theory of organizational ecological evolution via variations in cultural births and selection by deaths makes no predictions of events or processes that call into question any terms, concepts, or descriptions found within the organizational behavior analysis literature. Rather, it simply describes how individual organizational metacontingencies depend critically on their relations to an organizational ecology. And, it suggests (1) that probabilities (rates) of cultural foundings and deaths are statistically predictable when critical parameters in the quantitative portions of the theory can be estimated and (2) that top-level decision makers are part of a larger and more powerful process than any one person can alter. For example, a CEO may, in conjunction with other executives, decide that a new technology requires an investment while funding depends on approval by a board of directors and adoption and support of the new technology among those who work with the technology. No matter how high up in an organizational decision making hierarchy, one person alone cannot alter the process. Consequently, the organizational ecologists' account of organizational cultural evolution is resisted by those who would attribute organizational actions to a few key decision makers.

Why these decision makers make the decisions they do is directly related to the social and nonsocial contingencies that govern their decisions. These contingencies are in part to be found in the evolving competitive environment and individual decision makers' reinforcement histories. Not surprisingly, then, the point of contact between organizational behavior analysis and organizational ecology is the description of natural environmental processes responsible for selection among organizational metacontingencies for survival or death. If organizational behavior analysts are to better understand why top-level decision makers do what they do, then they must consider the personal reinforcement histories of individual decision makers as well as the history of the organizational culture in which the individual is situated and the competitive environment with which the organization must cope to survive.

One need not go into the statistical aspects of organizational ecology to establish a prima facia case concerning its validity as an account of cultural evolution. Rather, an important linkage between the organizational behavior analytic vantage point and organizational ecology vantage point is a mutual conviction that processes of evolution, whether at the level of an operant response or an entire culture, are seen in the evolution of interactions between the organism (via operant behavior) or the organization (cultural metacontingencies) and their respective environments.

ORGANIZATIONAL CULTURAL EVOLUTION BY METACONTINGENCY SELECTION AND REPLACEMENT IN THE AUTO INDUSTRY: EVOLUTIONARY HISTORY OF THE BIG THREE

The historical evolution of the auto industry exemplifies the evolutionary process of adaptation as replacement by cultural births and deaths, as selection against survival based on profit/loss metacontingencies. The evolutionary process is depicted in Figures 1 and 2. Figure 2 provides names of organizations, decades of their foundings, and decades of their death or absorption into other cultures. Figure 1 provides a simple graphical representation of the historical process and permits one to see eras when birth rates were rising, when death rates were rising, and the era characterized by falling birth rates and continued deaths and consolidations by mergers. Merged organizations are not counted as deaths; therefore, the picture might differ if mergers were treated as deaths. Also, the statistical vantage point does not provide information about the degree to which one or another organizational culture influenced metacontingencies of the aggregated culture. In order to obtain this information cultural histories would include descriptions of cultural practices and metacontingencies before and after mergers and acquisitions.

However, the competitive environment evolved in the direction of oligopolistic competition, few sellers and many buyers (Adams, 1986; Greer, 1984). This can be seen in the figures showing the dramatically falling number of car companies over time since the 1930s. In recent times the industry has been one characterized by rising prices in the face of falling market shares, at least for GM. Not considered here is the emerging network of relationships among U.S. and Japanese car companies and unions (Adams, 1986). The networks may eventually influence variations in cultures due to interactions among older U.S. and different Japanese practices. These, however, may be some of the most interesting developments which will determine the evolutionary direction of the industry from this time forward.

The main point of this presentation has not been to judge the efficacy of current or past practices in the industry. It is to show that the process of organizational cultural evolution involves variations among organizational cultures by some initial rate of births from which surviving cultures are shaped by a selection process which extinguishes (kills) the metacontingencies of some cultures, even though others may thrive. Selection against cultural survival is based on organizational cultural practices and related technological and financial structures or *survival-related metacontingencies*. Within a competitive population ecology individual organizations interact with other cultures and the disbanding of one culture in the population changes the metacontingencies of those which remain. The process is clearly evident in the population record of the auto industry. This particular record suggests that the industry is in a new phase with only three domestic auto companies in the population. But, the population ecology is changing because foreign competitors have entered it. The entry of these new competitors is a topic worthy of attention in its own right. Whether disbanding of one culture is "good" or "bad" for the surviving cultures in a population depends largely on the developmental stage of the ecology when disbanding occurs (Hannan & Freeman, 1989).

In brief, the decline of GM resembles that of U.S. Steel at another earlier time (Adam, 1986). It may not seem so, but if the descriptive net is cast wide enough, developments in "big steel" and the Big Three may provide data concerning a potential replication, i.e., answering the question whether common practices and common evolutionary histories produce the same, replicated, results. Is the auto industry collapsing? While the replication may not be perfect, it is analogous to the extent that technological and cultural inertia were followed by serious organizational declines in both cases.

DISCUSSION AND CONCLUSIONS

Whether top-level organizational leaders have the power to change the course of organizational cultural evolution once it has passed some critical point seems questionable if the course of events in "big steel" presage the course of events among the Big Three. As long as the evidence concerning predictability of a risky evolutionary path cannot be discriminated, there will always be resistance to behavioral and technological innovations (e.g., those now in place in the Saturn Corporation) which might reduce the risks of organizational decline and death. Organizational ecology (Hannan & Freeman, 1989) suggests that with a long enough temporal vantage point, the evolutionary game becomes rather probabilistic; to build cultures which will be long lived are attempts to beat odds stacked against ultimate success. Thus, the organizational behavior-analytic position is to consider whether methods can be employed to learn how to provide organizations with better cultural practices. Improved practices would provide a measure of insurance against some risks that flexible metacontingencies can produce utilizing certain types of wage/incentive systems (Redmon & Agnew, 1991). To investigate the evolutionary history of a particular organizational ecology is to learn whether there are exceptions to the rules of cultural evolution across cultures or if within cultures there exist cultural practices that operate like a gene in a human–a gene which might insure long life absent some accident.

In retrospect, organizational cultural inertia helps explain why very effective behavior technologies are not adopted by existing cultures as cultural innovations (see Geller, *JABA*, *24* (3), 1991, pp. 401-458). Both organizational ecology (Hannan & Freeman, 1989) and the histories of individual organizational cultural innovations (Handlin, 1992; Lincoln, 1946) suggest that innovations are more likely to occur in the early years of a newly founded culture when the organizational competitive environment can still be influenced by behavior of a single culture. For example, once the traditional conflicts between labor and management (Jermier, 1988) are formalized by competing organizational cultures with sometimes conflicting interests (Adams, 1986), resulting inflexibility in specific organizational cultures may set the stage for the type of cultural inertia which leads to decline and death. A critical question is whether these evolutionary paths must be repeated in industry after industry or whether different evolutionary paths are possible. If so, how does one guide an organizational ecology on such a course? One thing the organizational ecology position makes abundantly clear is that the fate of each organizational culture is intimately related to its overall competitive environment.

It is important to note that metacontingencies include not only cultural practices and their outcomes, but the individual histories of the people who populate the organizational culture. Top-level decision makers who develop, select, and attempt to implement organizational policies, strategies, and tactics are also part of the organization's metacontingencies. From this, other considerations follow: To the extent that members have been conditioned to respond to the environment in the traditional ways of the organizational culture, they can be expected to contribute to cultural inertia; To the extent that promotions are made from within a system that may be political, individuals who rise toward top jobs will support the culture and contribute to cultural inertia; To the extent that the organization has built into its culture support for rates of cultural and technological change correlated with rates of change among competitors in its competitive environment, cultural inertia will facilitate organizational survival; To the extent that the cultural practices within the organization resist or impede rates of cultural and technological change required by the rates of change among competitors and in their competitive environment, the organizational culture's survival-related metacontingencies will deteriorate and it will be at risk of death.

Society as a whole may not suffer greatly from the evolution of cultures within an industry by a process of cultural replacement via deaths and births. However, this will be little consolation to individuals who suffer major interruptions in their lives as the process of selection by consequences works upon variations among organizational cultural practices provided by a supply of new organizational births. Whether disruptive consequences of this amoral natural evolutionary process can be mitigated with the assistance of research by organizational behavior analysts will depend largely on whether these analysts recognize that the evolutionary process is operating, how it operates, and whether organizations can develop cultural practices which mitigate these potential threats to survival.

Redmon and Agnew (1991) have already made suggestions concerning how to construct more flexible financial metacontingencies. Following Gilbert's (1978) lead, they focus attention on improving "accomplishments that are worthy in terms of organization missions" (Redmon & Agnew, 1991, p. 138). It is essential, however, to go beyond this important first step. Whether top level decision makers are able to identify those missions which will prevent them from jeopardizing long-term maintenance of metacontingencies to achieve short-term objectives must be considered. If other portions of the culture are excluded from the analysis, having flexible metacontingencies such as those associated with the incentive pay system in Lincoln Electric Company (Handlin, 1992) will not suffice. For example, a drive for cost reductions with no benefits to customers is just as likely to attract competitors as is a high production cost structure. If an organization adopts a low cost low price orientation to its markets and dominates these markets (drives out competition), the double edged sword of cultural inertia is then required to keep the practices in place in the absence of competition. Consequently, when major shifts in the environment occur, inertia exposes the culture to the risk of death.

A new research agenda is required to encompass the social and economic contingencies of top-level decision makers as they deliberate about how to build organizational cultures (Eubanks & Lloyd, 1992) which contribute to optimizing the sometimes conflicting goals of economic progress, employment security (Greer, 1984), and employment growth (Weitzman, 1984). The discipline of organizational behavior analysis is uniquely positioned to advance research which links cultural anthropology, organizational cultural evolution, organizational ecology, Gaia, and behavior analyses. When the vantage points of each field are integrated, a more comprehensive vantage point will be achieved. The comprehensive vantage point will examine the social or cultural or material contingencies which account for top level decision makers' attempts to shape organizational cultures subject to environmental constraints. A multidisciplinary framework presents organizational behavior analysts with a variety of challenging research questions worthy of their best efforts and attention.

REFERENCES

Adams, W. (1986). *The structure of American industry.* (Seventh Edition), New York: Macmillan Publishing.

Baum, W. M. (1989). Quantitative prediction and molar description of the environment. *The Behavior Analyst, 12,* 167-176.

Cohen, H. L., & Filipczak, J. (1989). *A New Learning Environment.* Boston: Authors Cooperative.

Daft, R. L., & Weick, K. E. (1984). Toward a model of organizations as interpretive systems. *Academy of Management Review, 9* (2), 284-295.

Davis, S. M., & Lawrence, P. R. (1977). *Matrix.* Reading, MA: Addison-Wesley.

Eubanks, J. L., & Lloyd, K. E. (1992). Relating behavior analysis to the organizational culture concept and perspective. *Journal of Organizational Behavior Management, 12* (2).

Geller, E. S. (Ed.) (1991). *Journal of Applied Behavior Analysis, 24* (3), 401-458.

Gilbert, T. F. (1978). *Human competence: Engineering worthy performance.* New York: McGraw-Hill.

Glenn, S. S. (1988). Contingencies and metacontingencies: Toward a synthesis of behavior analysis and cultural materialism. *The Behavior Analyst, 11,* 161-179.

Glenn, S. S. (1991). Contingencies and metacontingencies: Relations among behavioral, cultural, and biological evolution. In P. A. Lamal (Ed.) *Behavioral analysis of societies and cultural practices* (pp. 39-73). Washington, D.C.: Hemisphere.

Gould, S. J. (1983). *Hen's teeth and horses' toes: Further reflections in natural history.* New York: W. W. Norton & Company.

Greer, D. F. (1984). *Industrial organization and public policy.* New York: Macmillan.

Handlin, H. C. (1992). The company built upon the golden rule: Lincoln Electric. In B. L. Hopkins & T. C. Mawhinney (Eds.) *Pay for performance: History, controversy, and evidence.* New York: The Haworth Press, Inc.

Hannan, M. T., & Freeman, J. (1989). *Organizational ecology.* Cambridge, MA: Harvard University Press.

Harris, M. (1979). *Cultural materialism.* New York: Random House.

Hedberg, B. (1981). How organizations learn and unlearn. In Paul C. Nystrom & William H. Starbuck (Eds.) (1981a). *Handbook of organizational design, volume I: Adapting organizations to their environments* (pp. 3-27). New York: Oxford University Press.

Herrnstein, R. J. (1990). Rational choice theory. *American Psychologist, 44* (2), 356-367.

Jermier, J. M. (1988). Sabotage at work: The rational view. In S. B. Bacharach & N. DiTomaso (Eds.), *Research in the sociology of organizations, 6.* Greenwich, Connecticut: JAI Press.

Kerr, S., & Slocum, J. W., Jr. (1981). Controlling the performance of people in organizations. In Paul C. Nystrom & William H. Starbuck (Eds.) (1981a).

Handbook of organizational design, volume II: Remodeling organizations and their environments (pp. 116-134). New York: Oxford University Press.

Lincoln, J. F. (1946). *Lincoln's incentive system.* New York: McGraw-Hill.

Lovelock, J. (1988). *The ages of gaia: A biography of our living earth.* New York: W. W. Norton.

Malagodi, E. F. (1986). On radical behaviorism: A call for cultural analysis. *The Behavior Analyst, 9,* 1-17.

Malott, R. W. (in press). A theory of rule-governed behavior and organizational behavior management. *Journal of Organizational Behavior Management, 12* (2).

March, J. G., and Simon, H. A. (1958). *Organizations.* New York: John Wiley & Sons.

Mawhinney, T. C. (1975). Operant terms and concepts in the description of individual work behavior: Some problems of interpretation, application, and evaluation. *Journal of Applied Psychology, 60,* 704-712.

Mawhinney, T. C. (1982). Maximizing versus matching in people versus pigeons. *Psychological Reports, 50,* 267-281.

Mawhinney, T. C., & Gowen, C. R., III. (1990). Gainsharing and the law of effect as the matching law: A theoretical framework. *Journal of Organizational Behavior Management, 11,* 61-75.

Melcher, A. J. (1976). *Structure and process of organizations: A systems approach.* Englewood Cliffs, N.J.: Prentice-Hall.

Miller, J. G. (1978). *Living systems.* New York: McGraw-Hill.

Mizruchi, M. S. (1983). Who controls whom? An examination of the relationship between management and boards of directors in large American corporations. *Academy of Management Review, 8* (3), 426-435.

Moxley, R. A. (1989). Some historical relationships between science and technology with implications for behavior analysis. *The Behavior Analyst, 12* (1), 45-57.

Organ, D. W., & Bateman, T. S. (1991). *Organizational behavior.* Homewood, IL: Irwin.

Nystrom, P. C., & Starbuck, W. H. (Eds.) (1981a). *Handbook of organizational design, volume I: Adapting organizations to their environments.* New York: Oxford University Press.

Nystrom, P. C., & Starbuck, W. H. (Eds.) (1981b). *Handbook of organizational design, volume II: Remodeling organizations and their environments.* New York: Oxford University Press.

Othersen, M. J., & Othersen, H. B., Jr. (1987). A history of hand washing: Seven hundred years at a snail's pace. *Pharos, 50* (2), 23-27.

Peach, E. B., & Wren, D. A. (1992). Pay for performance from antiquity to the 1950s. In B. L. Hopkins & T. C. Mawhinney (Eds.) *Pay for performance: History, controversy, and evidence.* New York: The Haworth Press, Inc.

Rachlin, H. (1989). *Judgement, decision, and choice.* New York: W. H. Freeman.

Redmon, W. K., & Agnew, J. L. (1991). Organizational behavior analysis in the United States: A view from the private sector. In P. A. Lamal (Ed.) *Behavior-*

al analysis of societies and cultural practices (pp. 125-139). Washington, D.C.: Hemisphere.

Skinner, B. F. (1953). *Science and human behavior.* New York: Macmillan.

Skinner, B. F. (1968). *The technology of teaching.* New York: Appleton-Century-Crofts.

Skinner, B. F. (1969). *Contingencies of reinforcement: A theoretical analysis.* New York: Appleton-Century-Crofts.

Skinner, B. F. (1981). Selection by consequences. *Science, 213,* 31 July, 501-504.

Sulzer-Azaroff, B., Pollack, M. J., & Fleming, R. K. (1992). Organizational behavior within structural and cultural constraints: An example from the human service sector. *Journal of Organizational Behavior Management, 12* (2).

Thompson, J. D. (1967). *Organizations in action: Social science bases of administrative theory.* New York: McGraw-Hill.

Weitzman, M. (1984). *The share economy: Conquering stagflation.* Cambridge, MA: Harvard University Press.

Zemke, R. E., & Gunkler, J. W. (1982). Organization-wide intervention. In L. W. Frederiksen (Ed.). *Handbook of organizational behavior management* (pp. 565-583). New York: Wiley.

Relating Behavior Analysis
to the Organizational Culture Concept
and Perspective

James L. Eubanks
Kenneth E. Lloyd

SUMMARY. The management and organization development communities have exhibited considerable interest in what are called the "organizational culture concept" and "organizational culture perspective." The concept vs. perspective approaches differ in important ways, particularly with respect to the collection and interpretation of data from organizations. The concept approaches to organizational culture are examined first. One concept approach with its foundations in cultural anthropology has captured the attention of behavior analysts, who have written about the connections among behavior analysis and the "cultural materialism" of Marvin Harris. The research biases of the organizational culture perspective are then discussed, along with their implications for changing organizational cultures. An organizational culture perspective approach emphasizing empirical investigation of social behavior characteristics is advocated and some of these characteristics are discussed in terms of how they can guide development of behavior analytic research and culture change programs.

Interest in culture is evident within organizational behavior management (Mawhinney, 1990) and within behavior analysis in general (Glenn, 1991; Pennypacker, 1987; Skinner, 1948, 1961, 1969). This interest has

James L. Eubanks and Kenneth E. Lloyd are affiliated with Central Washington University.

The order of authorship was assigned alphabetically. Neither author claims primacy or seniority. Reprint requests may be addressed to either author, Department of Psychology, Central Washington University, Ellensburg, WA 98926.

been further stimulated by the cultural anthropologist, Marvin Harris (1977, 1979, 1985, 1987). Reviews of his publications are in behavioral journals (Lloyd, 1985; Lloyd & Eubanks, 1989; Vargas, 1985) and he has presented papers at the Association for Behavioral Analysis meetings (Glenn, 1991; Harris, 1986; Pennypacker, 1987).

Extensions of behavior analytic principles to cultural phenomena have emphasized contingency analysis (Glenn, 1988), rule-governed behavior (Malott, 1988), and cultural design to address global issues (Malagodi, 1986; Malagodi & Jackson, 1989). A ten year review of the *Journal of Organizational Behavior Management* concluded that, while the journal has produced an archive of behavioral change data in organizations, ". . . we have yet to investigate very large scale interventions in which behavioral principles are employed to change the 'cultural foundations' of an organization" (Balcazar, Shupert, Daniels, Mawhinney, & Hopkins, 1989, p. 36).

Independent of this interdisciplinary interest has been an introduction of cultural concepts by the management and organization development (M/OD) communities to the study of organizational behavior (e.g., Deal & Kennedy, 1982; Ouchi, 1979, 1980; Ott, 1989; Peters & Waterman, 1982; Saffold, 1988; Uttal, 1983; Wiener, 1988; Wilkins & Dyer, 1988). The interest in organizational culture derives largely from its presumed impact on effectiveness. Although reports linking culture to organizational success have received widespread attention (cf. Peters & Waterman, 1982), the underlying evidence is weak (Wilkins, 1983). Peters and Waterman (1982) examined cultural characteristics of successful companies but failed to examine unsuccessful firms to determine if the cultural attributes were absent. The opposite and more desirable design of looking first at cultural characteristics and then at their success seems not to have been done.

CONCEPT VS. PERSPECTIVE APPROACHES

Our discussion of organizational culture closely follows that of Ott (1989, pp. 2-3, 67-69)) who distinguishes the culture concept from the culture perspective. According to this distinction, the concept approach to the study of organizational culture is largely nonempirical and intraverbal, emphasizing terms borrowed from cultural anthropology such as rites, rituals, artifacts, myths, and the like. The perspective approach, on the other hand, emphasizes *how* behavioral scientists should proceed in studying organizational culture. While emphasizing methodology, the perspective approach within the M/OD literature is still largely nonempirical (see Implications for Behavior Analysis below).

THE ORGANIZATIONAL CULTURE CONCEPT

The concept approach to organizational culture appears in the M/OD literature under many guises: organizational climate (Taguiri & Litwin, 1968), rules of the game (Schein, 1968; 1978); Van Maanen, 1976; 1979; Ritti & Funkhouser, 1982), organizational character (Harrison, 1972), or work group norms (Homans, 1950). Interest in a culture concept accelerated in the M/OD literature when two journals, *Administrative Science Quarterly* and *Organizational Dynamics* devoted entire issues to the topic in 1983. From January 1983 to July 1988 the M/OD literature listed 1029 separate citations which included organizational culture or corporate culture as key words (ABI Business Periodicals Index).

The resulting definition of organizational culture has been summarized as the pattern of values, beliefs, and expectations shared by the organization members (Huse & Cummings, 1990). Culture represents the taken-for-granted assumptions that people make about how work is to be done and evaluated and how employees relate to each other and significant others, such as customers, suppliers, and government agencies. The values and beliefs of organization members interact with a company's structure, control systems, and people to produce common norms about how members should behave.

Organizational culture, according to the concept approach, remains outside conscious awareness. It is the product of long-term social learning, reflecting what has worked in the past and what has been passed on to succeeding generations of employees to provide members with clear and widely shared answers to such practical questions as: Who's who and what matters around here? Who's us? Who's them? How do we treat us and them? How do we do things around here? What constitutes a problem and what do we do when one arises? What really matters around here and why? (Louis, 1982, cited in Huse & Cummings, 1990).

According to the M/OD literature, organizations in many industries, such as banking, energy, and electronics, have been facing complex and changing environments, including recession, deregulation, technological revolutions, foreign competition, and unpredictable markets. Many firms, such as AT&T, Pepsico, and Chase Manhattan have attempted to adapt to these conditions by changing business strategy and moving into new, unfamiliar areas. When efforts to implement a new strategy founder, the tendency is to attribute this failure to the unsuitability of the organization's culture to the new business (Deal & Kennedy, 1982; Peters & Waterman, 1982; Schein, 1985). An organizational culture that was once a source of strength for a company, the concept approach within the M/OD literature posits, can become a major liability in successfully implementing a new business strategy.

THE ORGANIZATIONAL CULTURE PERSPECTIVE

The organizational culture perspective, in contrast to the concept approach delineated above, emphasizes a methodology for studying culture. The M/OD literature, within the perspective approach, assumes that behavior in organizations cannot be studied using traditional research methods (e.g., Cook & Campbell, 1979). Instead methods more amenable for identifying or measuring ". . . unconscious, virtually forgotten basic assumptions concerning how things are done around here" is needed (Ott, 1989, p. 99). The alternatives most generally proposed are qualitative research methods such as ethnography and participant observation.

Within the M/OD perspective, a primary research principle is "first-hand inspection of ongoing organizational life" (Van Maanen, Dabbs, & Faulkner, 1982, p. 16, cited in Ott, 1989, pp. 102-103). Four other principles mentioned are:

1. *Analytic induction.* Patterns and generalizations are built from specific data. Data are not used to confirm or test pre-existing theories.
2. *Proximity.* Events and things must be witnessed firsthand. Second-hand accounts are not valid data. Thus, the organizational culture perspective does not permit interviews, questionnaires, and surveys.
3. *Ordinary behavior.* The perspective approach to organizational culture emphasizes routine, uninterrupted activities. Disruptions of routines, including those caused by research activities, distort data and are to be avoided. Data collection must be unobtrusive.
4. *Descriptive focus.* The first priority for organizational culture research is to describe what is going on in a given place at a certain time. This purpose is more important than explaining or predicting. (Van Maanen et al., p. 16; cited in Ott, 1989, pp. 102-103).

Few behavioral science research studies satisfy all these criteria. Only participant observation with the observer, or the observer's identity, concealed and archival data would fully meet these requirements.

The organizational culture perspective of the M/OD literature also addresses the changing of basic unconscious assumptions about what constitutes success (Ott, 1989, pp. 4-5). Frequently cited examples in this literature relate to desired cultural change at AT&T and Chrysler. AT&T had to change its assumptions about the value of technical superiority, and their "rightful dominance" in the telecommunications market. Similarly, Chrysler Corporation was considered a loser by its stockholders and assumed to be no longer competitive. The organizational culture perspective is assumed to be especially useful for describing behavior in organizations that are facing fundamental change in their identities (Ott, 1989, p. 2). Although the M/OD literature concerning the perspective approach consistently refers to cultural change, it is a changing environment beyond a specific organizational culture that is usually discussed. Changing the behavior of persons within a given culture which is experiencing this overall environmental change is not often discussed. Functional definitions are addressed (cf. Ott, 1989, p. 69) but they are dismissed in favor of more cognitive terminology.

In spite of the assertion by organizational culture perspective advocates of the unique suitability of their approach to organizational change, the M/OD literature remains ambivalent to its prospects for successful cultural change. Conflicting views range from whether a manager should even attempt to change organizational culture because of potential harmful effects (Schein, 1985) to arguments about which strategy to use. Some propose changing organizational culture by changing behavioral norms (Allen & Kraft, 1982), while others postulate that chief executive officers are the gate keepers of organizational culture (Davis, 1984). Equivocation toward the ethics of change and strategies for change are attributed to the relative infancy of the organizational culture perspective (Ott, 1989, p. 6), and the lack of grounding in systematic theory and research in the M/OD literature (Sathe, 1985, p. 1).

IMPLICATIONS FOR BEHAVIOR ANALYSIS

As described in the M/OD literature, organizational culture is essentially a cognitive concept. It is defined in terms of values, beliefs, expectations, and assumptions which are themselves inferred cognitive concepts. Hierarchies of inference have not been a part of behavior analysis. For the M/OD literature such inferred concepts are causal factors producing specific normative responses of organization members. For behavior analysts these inferred concepts (such as culture or value) are verbal labels (emitted by organization members) which are occasioned by responses of other organizational members (e.g., slogans, logos, dress, company picnics, etc.). Dramatic empirical evidence supporting this labeling process is available within social psychology (cf. Nisbett & Wilson, 1977). Although such labeling is attributed to "a priori causal theories," the data indicate that observers explain responses of others in terms of commonly acquired cliches.

It seems that the term, culture, is frequently emitted when an observer sees people from different organizations behaving differently. Behavior analysts would have no difficulty in accounting for responses peculiar to particular groups of people, i.e., different reinforcement histories can operate with members of different groups as well as they can with different individuals. From the organizational culture perspective, this is insufficient: culture is an unobservable, causal entity employed after the fact to "explain" different responses either verbal, nonverbal, social or nonsocial, rather than a descriptive term for observable social behavior.

These distinctions illustrate the extreme difficulty in making a transition from the organizational culture concept and perspective in the M/OD literature to behavior analysis. One such transition (Gilbert, 1978) relies upon levels of vantage points to indicate a hierarchy of outlooks varying from observation of behavior to comments on culture. A similar descriptive approach within this transition consists of reinterpreting the culture concept into a behavioral framework, e.g., Glenn (1988) and Malott (1988). All of these authors emphasize the culture concept from within a larger social context than is typically embraced by the organizational culture literature.

A second illustration of a possible transition from the M/OD literature to behavior analysis might be to reinterpret existing studies into behavioral principles. One such translation is entitled, "The Vicos Project: A Cross-Cultural Test of Psychological Propositions" (Kunkel, 1986). Vicos is an Andean hacienda (with village and inhabitants) which came under the direction of Cornell University anthropologists who introduced many reforms which in effect produced favorable and relatively immediate consequences for productive behaviors of the rural population in areas of agriculture, small businesses and services, education, and community affairs. The anthropologists described their procedures and interpreted their results in cognitive terms. Kunkel, in turn, translated their procedures into behavioral terms. The fit (of the actual procedures used by the anthropologists) with behavior analysis is remarkable. In this instance the anthropologists described their procedures in considerable detail; such detail is either missing or only broadly mentioned in reports of organizational cultural change. Attempts to replicate Kunkel's translation with organizational culture reports would require considerable guessing.

Kunkel reinterpreted a particular set of behavior change procedures implemented within a long-term study. A different reinterpretation procedure would be to compare research methods described and advocated by organizational culture perspectives with those actually employed in behavior analysis. The most explicit research methods available are those of Van Maanen et al. (1982) cited above. Their primary consideration of "first hand inspection" is compatible with direct observation of behavior, as well as immediate and frequent recording procedures advocated by organizational behavior analysts (Komaki, 1986; O'Brien, Dickinson, & Rosow, 1982). Both "analytic induction" and "proximity" fit with direct observation and close adherence to data rather than relying on pre-existing theory. While "ordinary behavior" aligns with event recording, neither organizational culture nor behavior analysis strictly meet the requirement of unobtrusive measurement. Reactive effects of baseline recording often remain unknown. The behavior analytic reliance on informed consent is partly assumed to alter unobtrusiveness.

Finally, "descriptive focus" seems to fit with baseline data routinely collected by behavior analysts. The methods advocated by Van Maanen et al. (1982) do not address procedures for changing culture. Instead they focus on collecting data from existing organizational practices. Reinterpretations, albeit interesting, are not a satisfactory transition from organizational culture to behavior analysis. Any reinterpretation is weak as long as we lack mutually acceptable criteria for evaluating different reinterpretations.

Still a third transition would introduce organizational culture terms into descriptions of straightforward behavior analyses. Two behavioral articles which do this are entitled, "Creating a reinforcing culture the HP way" (Frederick, 1986) and "Performance management in Great Britain: The differences are cultural" (Mosher, 1986). Seeing the term culture in a title might induce a reader to examine the article and thus be exposed to procedures which could prove helpful.

In a similar manner behavioral practitioners may find it useful when entering organizations to introduce their clients to change procedures with a description of cultural phenomena. A client who has just completed a weekend organizational culture workshop will not likely be viewing behavior in relation to its antecedents and consequences. She is going to want a new culture for her organization. The behavioral consultant must be prepared to speak a language compatible with this client. These issues confronting a behavior analyst encountering the organizational culture perspective are not unlike parallel issues (e.g., cognitive psychology) being discussed in the behavioral literature (Deitz & Arrington, 1983; Hineline, 1980; Lee, 1987; Neuringer, 1991; Pierce & Epling, 1984).

None of these transitions (reinterpretations, changing terms, adding new ones), either together or singly, seems entirely satisfactory. They neither stress an empirical approach nor emphasize the methodological skills possessed by behavior analysts for analyzing and changing behavior.

CHANGE IS THE BUSINESS OF BEHAVIOR ANALYSIS

Describing and carrying out procedures for changing behavior is an immediate contribution behavior analysts can make to organizations seeking change. While the organizational culture perspective may lack confidence and data on changing organizational behavior, behavior analysis is particularly well suited to attack this problem (Balcazar et al., 1989). Given our existing change technologies, the question remains whether the organizational culture concept and/or perspective are useful for addressing behavior change.

Despite the use of such terms as ethnography, values, beliefs, artifacts, and rituals, the organizational culture concept is not based on an anthropological framework. Although anthropologists may serve as consultants to corporations contemplating change (Uttal, 1983), the anthropological literature is not seriously cited (Allaire & Firsirotu, 1984, pp. 193-195). Occasionally an anecdote about Navajo or Inuit behavior (Ott, 1989, p. 20) is inserted, but only tangentially. Similarly, the social psychological literature on values, attitudes, and beliefs is not seriously examined.

Anthropology, with its historical and descriptive emphasis based on observing social groups, is probably not a good perspective with respect to behavior change. Certainly the notion of changing culture or behavior is not a central theme in anthropology (but see Kunkel, 1986, for an exception). Widely recognized anthropological topics such as cultural universals, acculturation, family and kinship structure, or use of resources in controlling the means of production or reproduction (Harris, 1979,

p. 46) are absent in the organizational culture literature. Training programs for new organization members are mentioned, but they are not related to anthropological accounts of acculturation, child rearing or initiation ceremonial practices.

Instead, the consistent emphasis in the M/OD literature related to organizational culture is on listening and talking with employees at all levels, administering questionnaires and surveys, or conducting three to five-day workshops in a retreat setting to change attitudes and beliefs. Whether any of these procedures generalize to the work place or change any behavior of employees is seldom discussed. This reliance upon verbal interactions among employees mirrors much of the mainstream social science literature (including psychology). However, even some anthropologists shy away from this source of data. The cultural materialist (Harris, 1979) analyzes the infrastructure of a culture (i.e., modes of production and reproduction within the society) rather than concentrating on the verbal reports of the people. In Harris' view, verbal descriptions of cultural practices (their superstructure) evolved after (not before) the cultural practices were generated by infrastructural variables.

The organizational culture literature emphasizes a primacy for verbal behavior in controlling all other behavior in organizations. This assumed primacy of verbal behavior over other response classes may be the majority view in social science, but there are other authors besides Harris who question it. In social psychology Bem (1972) has advocated a change behavior-then-change attitude hypothesis rather than the more prevalent change attitude-then-change behavior maxim. Serious questions regarding the controlling relations of cognitions over behavior have been examined and empirically tested by social psychologists (Nisbett & Wilson, 1977). Within behavior analysis the study of say-do and say-say relationships suggest that any relationship (including none) may exist between verbal responses and other response classes (Lloyd, 1980; Risley & Hart, 1968). Similarly, the issue regarding whether covert vs. overt verbal behaviors enjoy causal status over behavioral processes has been addressed by behavior analysts (cf. Chase, 1991). All of this literature is either unknown or ignored within the organizational culture perspective.

From a behavioral point of view, the organizational culture perspective is a nonheuristic approach. It is simply not sufficiently specific to permit empirical evaluation. But an empirical evaluation is not a criterion for the acceptance of such a descriptive approach in the marketplace. Often description (without empirical evaluation) in organizational culture (as in social science generally) is accepted by consumers as equivalent to expla-

nation. We conclude that the culture concept as used in the M/OD literature is unproductive if not misleading (cf. Allaire & Firsirotu, 1984).

ANALYSIS OF SOCIAL BEHAVIOR
AND THE CULTURE CONCEPT

The remainder of our paper is a description of social behavior as it
may be relevant to the organizational culture concept. For this we are
indebted to Skinner's and Harris' comments on social behavior and culture. Neither author offers a functional definition of culture nor a detailed
behavior analysis of the topic. Instead they shift to specific features that
seem to constitute part of the culture concept, such as religion, education,
group control (e.g., Skinner, 1953, p. 323) or to specific features of cultural materialism (e.g., Harris, 1979, pp. 46-114). Our paper concentrates
on issues susceptible to an empirical examination regarding social behavior. Our issues are only some of those that seem relevant to the culture
concept.

The topic of culture requires an emphasis on social behavior as a
special case of analysis of behavior in general. Our comments on social
behavior overlap significantly with those offered by behavior analysts for
verbal behavior. Verbal behavior is the more neutral of the two terms;
social behavior admittedly carries more everyday notions, but it is certainly more compatible with an industrial/organizational psychology and
M/OD audiences. In either case, social or verbal, the response class of
interest is defined as those responses whose reinforcers are mediated by
the behaviors of other persons. Social behavior is contrasted with nonsocial behaviors whose reinforcers are directly contingent upon the responses within the class, i.e., one or more other persons are not needed
to arrange reinforcers. Such reinforcers, which follow non-social responses, are controlled by physical and biological factors in the environment.

Distinguishing response classes by the source of their reinforcers is
unusual in behavior analysis. Unlike mainstream psychology, behavior
analysis has not emphasized distinctions among categories of behavior,
i.e., not between, say, abnormal or normal, or between child or adult
behaviors. Responses typical of these familiar categories certainly differ,
but their functional relationships with the environment seem best described by the already familiar principles of behavior.

There are some exceptions to this general absence of behavioral categories within behavior analysis, e.g., escape and avoidance behaviors or
operant and respondent behaviors. But these response classes have been

distinguished by the procedures employed to identify and change them and not on the basis of the source of their reinforcers. Procedural features do not seem to separate social and nonsocial behaviors, i.e., reinforcers from any source would still follow responses closely in time, differential reinforcement would still be needed, stimulus control would be established, and so on.

The distinction based upon reinforcer source seems paramount. Yet it seems to leave much unsaid. Although important, the distinction is not entirely clear by itself. Some responses may be maintained by a combination of reinforcers mediated both by the physical environment and by other people. Perhaps we should refer to sources (plural), not simply source. In other cases it may not be possible or necessary to identify all the controlling reinforcers.

Behavior analysts have addressed the issue of reinforcer definition in terms of source dimensions. The issue of "intrinsic motivation," for example, and whether it is diminished by "extrinsic" reinforcement (cf. Deci, 1971, 1975) has been approached effectively using a functional analysis (Dickinson, 1989; Mawhinney, 1979; Scott, 1975). Similarly, a paradigm for separating multiple sources of reinforcer "value" has been devised using concurrent schedules (Mawhinney, Dickinson, & Taylor, 1989).

Most instances of human behavior would seem to be under multiple discriminative control of social and nonsocial conditions. Clearly more must be said. Whatever else is said, however, must be capable of empirical test. We end with a list of suggested characteristics of social behavior. They are untested generalizations from behavior analysis, from social psychology and other social sciences. They seem worthy of empirical study. An empirical approach could indicate their relative importance as well as point to additional testable characteristics.

SOME SUGGESTED CHARACTERISTICS OF SOCIAL BEHAVIOR

1. *Interlocking behaviors.* By definition, social behavior requires two or more people somehow exchanging reinforcers, i.e., each momentarily labeled a speaker or a listener. Their roles constantly shift from one to another. For example, a speaker who asks a question becomes a listener when the former listener starts to answer the question (thus becoming a speaker). Such interlocking behaviors involve the three term contingency between speakers and listeners. Most social behavior would likely be discriminated

in this manner (Skinner, 1957, p. 83 ff). Significant behavioral work has begun in this area, addressing social units and phenomena such as cooperation, competition, equity, altruism, leadership, and exchange behaviors (cf. Burgess & Bushell, 1969; Hake & Olvera, 1978; Marwell & Schmitt, 1975; Mawhinney & Ford, 1977; Rao & Mawhinney, 1991). Important as these beginnings are, however, a considerable amount of behavioral work remains to be done both in the lab and in the field to address the complex interactions among variables controlling social behavior (cf. Schmitt, 1986).

2. *Role switching.* The shifting of roles within interlocking behavior classes provided Skinner (1953, p. 323) with a rationale for how the group can control individual behavior, i.e., each individual is part of the group control process for all other individuals in the group at one time or another.

3. *Higher order contingencies.* A four-term contingency involving conditional probabilities (Lee, 1987; Sidman, 1986) seems appropriate for describing role shifting and interlocking social behaviors. Mainstream analyses of social behavior often refer to a global setting before describing some characteristic responses. Such analyses stop at the level of "one" or at best "two" terms in the contingencies, and the two-term model emphasizes events which precede (not follow) the target behaviors. These emphasized events may or may not be observable.

4. *Training programs.* A stable group of people must establish training programs to socialize new members. Particular responses of novices (children or new employees) will be reinforced in the presence of certain conditions. These responses may seem arbitrary when first observed (e.g., worshiping cows), but Harris (1977, p. 147) proposes to remove this appearance of arbitrariness by relating social behaviors to infrastructural variables within the group's environment.

5. *Reinforcer selection.* Conditional eliciting stimuli and reinforcers for social behavior are not only decided by the group, but the group and the environment arranges which particular events (social and nonsocial) will be reinforcers for that group. This latter feature has not been emphasized by behavior analysts, but is of great interest both to the cultural materialist and to the organizational culture perspective. We have particularly noted conditional eliciting stimuli since these are often unmentioned in a behavioral analysis yet are stressed in the M/OD literature.

6. *Reinforcer effectiveness.* In comparison to reinforcers for nonsocial behavior, social reinforcers are likely to be sloppily and intermittently delivered. Listeners do not necessarily discriminate their role as mediators of reinforcer effectiveness so that social reinforcers may not be contingent, immediate, of appropriate size, or related to satiation levels. Similarly, listeners may not detect relevant conditional eliciting stimuli or conditional responses for a speaker.

7. *Reinforcer distribution.* Within groups, many social reinforcers can and have ended up under the control of relatively few persons in the group. Behavior analysts have described counter-control procedures (Holland, 1985), along with behavioral aspects of social change and economic development (cf. Kunkel, 1969; Skinner, 1969) but little research is available (Stokes, Fowler, & Baer, 1978).

8. *Reinforcer restrictions.* The range of behaviors reinforced within a group setting may involve restrictions. If individuals in the group exceed these restrictions then their rewards may be larger or more immediate. This "tragedy of the commons" (Hardin, 1968) describes a social dilemma which begs an empirical analysis.

9. *Response class relationships.* Interactions among different response classes either within or between individuals become more relevant in groups, e.g., say-do, do-say, say-say, and "do-do" correspondences as noted above (cf. Lloyd, 1980).

10. *Research designs.* Methodologically, group research designs may be useful. Changing a group mean as opposed to changing responses of any one person may be easier and sometimes more desirable, e.g., where responses need only be measured once across many individuals as is the case with voters or jurists.

11. *Weak stimulus control.* Finally, as you patiently read on wondering when this article will end it must be noted that terminating social episodes can be awkward. When the last nail has been driven into a wooden fence we readily replace the hammer and move on to the next task. When leaving a social gathering or ending a manuscript we dawdle. So does our audience. Distinct cues such as those present when completing a fence are often absent in social circumstances.

Our list of suggested characteristics is incomplete and inaccurate without empirical verification which we hope can be undertaken. A more precise specification of culture (via social behavior) might both restrict its broad usage and facilitate its usefulness while interacting with other organizations and disciplines. Empirical knowledge of wide ranging characteristics of social behavior should strengthen the behaviorist's hand in discussions of culture.

REFERENCES

Administrative Science Quarterly, (1983). *28*, 331-500.

Allaire, Y., & Firsirotu, M. E. (1984). Theories of organizational culture. *Organization Studies, 5*, 193-226.

Allen, R., & Kraft, C. (1982). *The organizational unconscious: How to create the corporate culture you want and need.* Englewood Cliffs, NJ: Prentice-Hall.

Balcazar, F., Shupert, M., Daniels, A., & Hopkins, B. (1989). An objective review and analysis of ten years of publication in the Journal of Organizational Behavior Management. *Journal of Organizational Behavior Management, 10*, 7-38.

Bem, D. (1972). Self-perception theory. In L. Berkowitz (Ed.), *Advances in experimental social psychology.* New York: Academic Press.

Burgess, R. L., & Bushell, D., Jr. (1969). *Behavioral sociology: The experimental analysis of social processes.* New York: Columbia University Press.

Chase, P. N. (1991). Humble behaviorism or equal doses of skepticism? *The Behavior Analyst, 14*, 15-18.

Cook, T., & Campbell, D. (1979). *Quasi-experimentation: Design and analysis issues for field settings.* Boston: Houghton Mifflin.

Davis, S. (1984). *Managing corporate culture.* Reading, MA: Addison-Wesley.

Deal, T. E., & Kennedy, A. A. (1982). *Corporate cultures: The rites and rituals of corporate life.* Reading, MA: Addison-Wesley.

Deci, E. L. (1971). Effects of externally mediated rewards on intrinsic motivation. *Journal of Personality and Social Psychology, 18*, 105-115.

Deci, E. L. (1975). *Intrinsic motivation.* New York: Plenum.

Deitz, S. M., & Arrington, R. L. (1983). Factors confusing language use in the analysis of behavior. *Behaviorism, 11*, 117-132.

Dickinson, A. M. (1989). The detrimental effects of extrinsic reinforcement on "intrinsic motivation." *The Behavior Analyst, 12*, 1-15.

Frederick, L. (1986). Creating a reinforcing culture the HP way. *Performance Management Magazine, 4*, 14-16.

Gilbert, T. F. (1978). *Human competence: Engineering worthy performance.* New York: McGraw-Hill.

Glenn, S. S. (1988). Contingencies and metacontingencies: Toward a synthesis of behavior analysis and cultural materialism. *The Behavior Analyst, 11*, 161-180.

Glenn, S. S. (1991, May). *The integration of cultural materialism and behavior analysis.* Symposium conducted at the meetings of the Association for Behavior Analysis: International, Atlanta, GA.

Hake, D. F., & Olvera, E. (1978). Cooperation, competition, and related social phenomena. In A. C. Catania & T. A. Brigham (Eds.), *Handbook of Applied Behavior Analysis: Social and instructional processes.* New York: Irvington, 208-245.

Hardin, G. (1968). The tragedy of the commons. *Science, 162,* 1243-1248.

Harris, M. (1977). *Cannibals and kings: The origins of culture.* New York: Random House.

Harris, M. (1979). *Cultural materialism: The struggle for a science of culture.* New York: Random House.

Harris, M. (1985). *Good to eat: Riddles of food and culture.* New York: Simon Schuster.

Harris, M. (1986, May). *Cultural materialism and behavior analysis: Common problems and radical solutions.* Invited address presented at the meeting of the Association for Behavior Analysis: International, Milwaukee, WI.

Harris, M. (1987, May). Discussant. In H. S. Penneypacker (Chair), *Behavior analysis and cultural materialism.* Symposium conducted at the meetings of the Association for Behavior Analysis: International, Nashville, TN.

Harrison, R. (1972). Understanding your organization's character. *Harvard Business Review, 50,* 119-128.

Hineline, P. N. (1980). The language of behavior analysis: Its functions and its limitations. *Behaviorism, 8,* 67-86.

Holland, J. G. (1985, August). *Consecuencias politicas de aplicar la psicologia conductual.* Paper presented at the Simposio Peruano de Psicologia del Aprendizaje Aplicada a la Educacion, Arequipa, Peru.

Homans, G. (1950). *The human group.* New York: Harcourt-Brace.

Huse, E. F., & Cummings, T. G. (1990). *Organizational development and change.* (4th ed.). Los Angeles: West Publishing Company.

Komaki, J. (1986). Applied behavior analysis and organizational behavior: Reciprocal influence of the two fields. *Research in Organizational Behavior, 8,* 297-334.

Kunkel, J. H. (1969). Some behavioral aspects of social change and economic development. In R. L. Burgess & D. Bushell, Jr. (Eds.), *Behavioral sociology: The experimental analysis of social process.* New York: Columbia University Press.

Kunkel, J. H. (1986). The Vicos project: A cross-cultural test of psychological propositions. *The Psychological Record, 36,* 451-466.

Lee, V. L. (1987). The structure of conduct. *Behaviorism, 15,* 141-148.

Lloyd, K. E. (1980). Do as I say, not as I do. *New Zealand Psychologist, 9,* 1-8.

Lloyd, K. E. (1985). Behavioral anthropology: A review of Marvin Harris' Cultural Materialism. *Journal of the Experimental Analysis of Behavior, 43,* 279-287.

Lloyd, K. E., & Eubanks, J. L. (1989). Why nothing works in America now: A review of two books by Marvin Harris. *Journal of Organizational Behavior Management, 10,* 212-218.

Louis, M. (1982, April). *Toward a system of inquiry on organizational culture.* Paper presented at the Western Academy of Management Meeting, Colorado Springs, CO.

Marwell, G., & Schmitt, D. R. (1975). *Cooperation: An experimental analysis.* New York: Academic Press.

Mawhinney, T. C. (1979). Intrinsic X extrinsic motivation: Perspectives from behaviorism. *Organizational behavior and human performance, 24,* 411-440.

Mawhinney, T. C. (1990, May). *Rule-governed behavior, organizational cultures and OBM.* Symposium conducted at the meetings of the Association for Behavior Analysis: International, Nashville, TN.

Mawhinney, T. C., Dickinson, A. M., & Taylor, L. A., III. (1989). The use of concurrent schedules to evaluate the effects of extrinsic rewards on "intrinsic motivation." *Journal of Organizational Behavior Management, 10,* 109-129.

Mawhinney, T. C., & Ford, J. D. (1977). The path-goal theory of leadership: An operant interpretation. *Academy of Management Review, 2,* 398-411.

Malagodi, E. (1986). On radicalizing behaviorism: A call for cultural analysis. *The Behavior Analyst, 9,* 1-17.

Malagodi, E., & Jackson, K. (1989). Behavior analysts and cultural analysis: Troubles and issues. *The Behavior Analyst, 12,* 17-34.

Malott, R. W. (1988). Rule-governed behavior and behavioral anthropology. *The Behavior Analyst, 11,* 181-204.

Mosher, J. (1986). Performance management in Great Britain: The differences are cultural. *Performance Management Magazine, 4,* 34-36.

Neuringer, A. (1991). Humble behaviorism. *The Behavior Analyst, 14,* 1-14.

Nisbett, R. E., & Wilson, T. D. (1977). Telling more than we can know: Verbal reports on mental processes. *Psychological Review, 84,* 231-259.

O'Brien, R., Dickinson, A., & Rosow, M. (1982). *Industrial behavior modification: a management handbook.* New York: Pergamon Press.

Organizational Dynamics, 1983, Autumn, *13,* 1-64.

Ott, J. (1989). *The organizational culture perspective.* Pacific Grove: CA, Brooks/Cole.

Ouchi, W. G. (1979). *Theory Z: How American business can meet the Japanese challenge.* Reading, MA: Addison-Wesley.

Penneypacker, H. S. (1987, May). *Behavior analysis and cultural materialism.* Symposium conducted at the meetings of the Association for Behavior Analysis: International, Nashville, TN.

Peters, T., & Waterman, R. (1982). *In search of excellence.* New York: Harper & Row.

Pierce, D. W., & Epling, W. F. (1984). On the persistence of cognitive explanation: Implications for behavior analysis. *Behaviorism, 12,* 15-28.

Rao, R. K., & Mawhinney, T. C. (1991). Superior-subordinate dyads: Dependence of leader effectiveness on mutual reinforcement contingencies. *Journal of the Experimental Analysis of Behavior, 56,* 105-118.

Risley, T. R., & Hart, B. (1968). Developing correspondence between non-verbal and verbal behavior of pre-school children. *Journal of Applied Behavior Analysis, 1*, 267-281.

Ritti, R., L. & Funkhouser, G. (1982). *The ropes to skip and the ropes to know.* Columbus, OH; Grid.

Saffold, G. S., III. (1988). Culture traits, strength, and organizational performance: Moving beyond "strong" culture. *Academy of Management Review, 13*, 546-558.

Sathe, V. (1985). *Culture and related corporate realities: Text, cases, and readings on organizational entry, establishment, and change.* Homewood, IL: Irwin.

Schein, E. (1968). Organizational socialization and the profession of management. *Industrial Management Review, 9*, 1-15.

Schein, E. (1978). *Career dynamics: Matching individual and organizational needs.* Reading, MA: Addison-Wesley.

Schein, E. (1985). *Organizational culture and leadership: A dynamic view.* San Francisco: Jossey-Bass.

Scott, W. E., Jr. (1975). The effects of extrinsic rewards on "intrinsic motivation." *Organizational Behavior and Human Performance, 15*, 117-129.

Sidman, M. (1986). Functional analysis of emergent verbal classes. In T. Thompson & M. D. Zeiler (Eds.), *Analysis of behavioral units.* Hillsdale, NJ: Erlbaum, 213-245.

Skinner, B. F. (1948). *Walden two.* New York: Macmillan.

Skinner, B. F. (1953). *Science and human behavior.* New York: Macmillan.

Skinner, B. F. (1961). *Cumulative record.* New York: Appleton-Century-Crofts.

Skinner, B. F. (1969). *Contingencies of reinforcement: A theoretical analysis.* New York: Appleton-Century-Crofts.

Skinner, B. F. (1969). Contingencies of reinforcement in the design of a culture. In R. L. Burgess & D. Bushell, Jr. (Eds.). *Behavioral sociology: The experimental analysis of social process.* New York: Columbia University Press, 366-378.

Stokes, T. F., Fowler, S. A., & Baer, D. M. (1978). Training preschool children to recruit natural communities of reinforcement. *Journal of Applied Behavior Analysis, 11*, 285-303.

Taguiri, R., & Litwin, G. (1968). *Organizational climate: Exploration of a concept.* Boston: Harvard University Press.

Uttal, B. (1983). The corporate culture vultures. *Fortune, 17*, 66-72.

Van Maanen, J. (1976). Breaking in: Socialization to work. In R. Dubin (Ed.), *Handbook of work, organization, and society.* Chicago: Rand McNally.

Van Maanen, J. (1979). The fact of fiction in organizational ethnography. *Administrative Science Quarterly, 24*, 539-550.

Van Maanen, J., Dabbs, J. Jr., & Faulkner, R. (Eds). (1982). *Varieties of qualitative research.* Beverly Hills, CA: Sage Publications.

Vargas, E. A. (1985). Cultural contingencies: A review of Marvin Harris's "Cannibals and Kings." *Journal of the Experimental Analysis of Behavior, 43*, 419-428.

Wiener, Y. (1988). Forms of value systems: A focus on organizational effectiveness and cultural change and maintenance. *Academy of Management Review, 13*, 534-545.

Wilkins, A. L. (1983). Organizational stories as symbols which control the organization. In L. R. Pondy, P. J. Frost, G. Morgan, & T. C. Dandridge (Eds.), *Organizational symbolism.* Greenwich, CT: JAI Press.

Wilkins, A. L., & Dyer, W. G., Jr. (1988). Toward culturally sensitive theories of cultural change. *Academy of Management Review, 13*, 522-533.

TWO THEORIES
OF RULE-GOVERNED BEHAVIOR

A Theory of Rule-Governed Behavior
and Organizational Behavior
Management

Richard W. Malott

SUMMARY. To a large extent, an organization's culture is probably not based on direct-acting contingencies of reinforcement and
punishment. Instead it is generally based on indirect-acting contingencies (i.e., analog to reinforcement and punishment). A direct-
acting contingency is one where the outcome involved in the contingency is sufficiently immediate, sizable, and probable to reinforce
or punish the causal response. An indirect-acting contingency is one
that controls the causal response, though the outcome contingent on
that response is too improbable to actually reinforce or punish that
causal response. In cases where indirect-acting contingencies do
control the response, it seems likely that they do so through the actions of rules describing those contingencies; in other words, such
control is an instance of rule-governed behavior. Thus much of the
control exerted by an organization's culture is through rule governance.

Richard W. Malott is affiliated with Western Michigan University.

THE RULE-GOVERNED ANALOG TO REINFORCEMENT

Mawhinney (1975) pointed out a number of problems with inappropriate uses of operant terms and concepts in organizational behavior management. He also pointed to a role for rule governed behavior in this area. "A person who has experience with an environment may be able to verbalize the contingencies in it and therefore instruct another as to how to behave for S+ [reinforcement]. Behavior of the person so instructed is termed *rule governed*, whereas his instructor's behavior is termed *contingency shaped*" (p. 707).

Mawhinney and Ford (1977) elaborate more on the importance of rule-governed behavior and rule control in what we might label organizational culture: "We consider the role of the leader to be that of organizing, specifying, and maintaining complex response chains of subordinates by communicating to them the contingencies of reinforcement . . . in the work place. This is accomplished by verbal behavior and administration of leader controlled reinforcers.

"Because people are capable of verbal behavior, the SDs of a task situation can be learned by one person and passed on to others in the form of propositions . . . . [The leader does this] by telling them the rules of reinforcement . . . . The leader's role behavior is then rule generation and execution" (p. 406).

Mawhinney concludes his earlier paper on the problems of terminological and conceptual confusion (1975): "The point . . . has not been to solve the problems observed, but to simply point them out in the belief that the first step in problem solution is recognition of the problem." The present paper is merely a subsequent, tentative step along the path Mawhinney and Mawhinney and Ford began over fifteen years ago.

Coming from the tradition of the animal laboratory, behavior analysts typically analyze complex human behavior in terms of the direct-acting contingencies of reinforcement and punishment that so clearly operate in the laboratory (e.g., Weisberg and Waldrop's analysis of the "fixed-interval work habits of congress," 1972). (A *direct-acting contingency* is a contingency for which the outcome of the response reinforces or punishes that response.) But those direct-acting contingencies have analogs involving contingencies that are not direct-acting. Such contingencies will not reinforce or punish a response (e.g., when the outcome is too delayed). However, a rule describing such a contingency might control the relevant response. (Such a contingency is *indirect acting*—a contingency that controls behavior indirectly rather than through the direct action of reinforcement or punishment by the outcome in that contingency.)

These indirect-acting contingencies look like examples of reinforcement, except the reinforcers are, for example, too delayed. Such contingencies are *rule-governed analogs to reinforcement by the presentation of a reinforcer*–an increase in the likelihood of a response because of a rule stating the occasions, when the response will produce a reinforcer. (*By rule*, I mean, "a verbal description of a behavioral contingency"; this use is essentially the same as Skinner's in his introduction of the concept [Skinner, 1969, p. 157] and by *behavioral contingency*, I mean, "a response, an outcome, and a stimulus in the presence of which the response will produce that outcome" [Malott, 1989, p. 273].)

Most research in organizational behavior management uses procedures based on rule-governed analogs to direct-acting contingencies rather than procedures based on direct-acting contingencies themselves (Malott, Shimamune, & Malott, 1992). (Though there seems to be no relevant human literature, the nonhuman data generally suggest that reinforcers delayed by more than 60 seconds will not reinforce a response. For an intriguing exception, see Lett, 1973; and for a general discussion of so-called "delayed reinforcement" and of the anomaly of the bait-shy phenomenon or taste aversion, see Malott & Malott, 1991.)

AN EXAMPLE OF A RULE-GOVERNED ANALOG TO REINFORCEMENT

Brown, Malott, Dillon, and Keeps (1980) increased exceptional sales behavior (promptness, sociability, and courtesy), by telling the salespeople a rule describing the contingency between their earning the highest sales-skills rating and their winning a $25 certificate. The delay between the sales performance and the $25 reinforcer was too great for reinforcement (two weeks); so the exceptional sales behavior must have increased because the intervention contingency was a rule-governed, indirect-acting analog to reinforcement.

In this case, the rule statement directly controlled the behavior, but still the analog contingency might influence the extent to which that rule exerted control: If no one ever received a $25 certificate, there might well be a gradual drop in the frequency of exceptional sales behavior. Possibly the salespeople would develop counter-rules, based on the changed contingencies, in contradiction to the notion that false rules generate insensitivity to true contingencies (Matthews, Catania, & Shimoff, 1985). As Cerutti (1989, p. 260, 264-265) notes, "Insensitivity should not be considered a necessary property of rule-governed behavior."

DELAYED REINFORCERS AND SELF-MANAGEMENT

Normally, if two contingencies operate concurrently, the contingency with the more immediate outcome will more reliably control behavior (Chung, 1965; Chung & Herrnstein, 1967; Shimp, 1969). So most behavior analysts seem to agree that problems of self-management, and by extension, problems of performance management in general, result from the poor control exerted by delayed outcomes relative to immediate outcomes (Brown & Herrnstein, 1975, pp. 188-193; Logue, Peña-Correal, Rodriguez, & Kabela, 1986; Rachlin & Green, 1972). Ainslie (1975) also documented that this view of self-control is common in economics, sociology, social psychology, and dynamic psychology.

Behavior analysts cite such studies as Rachlin and Green's (1972) classic experiment where the pigeon more often pecked the key that produced an immediate but smaller reinforcer than the key that produced a delayed but larger reinforcer. They offered this as the paradigm of the self-management problem.

Though the data are sound, they may not be relevant to most problems of normal, adult human performance management, including self-management. In such studies, the delays between the response and the reinforcer were typically only a few seconds, or a minute or so, at the most; and potential learned reinforcers often intervened within that delay, possibly reinforcing the response. But, in many human situations, the delays are far too great for the outcome manipulated reinforcer to reinforce the measured response; and yet the indirect-acting, delayed contingency seems to exert more control than direct-acting, immediate contingencies (Braam & Malott, 1991; Brown et al., 1980).

Furthermore, in experiments structurally similar to Rachlin and Green's pigeon experiments, normal, verbal human beings state rules describing the contingencies and respond in a self-managed, rule-governed way, not in the pigeon's way; they select the larger, delayed reinforcers rather than the smaller, immediate reinforcers (Logue, Peña-Correal, Rodriguez, & Kabela, 1986).

Small but Cumulative Outcomes

If delayed outcomes do not cause poor self-management and the need for performance management, what does? The biggest problem may occur when an immediate outcome for each specific instance of a response class is too small to reinforce or punish that response class, though the cumulative impact of many such outcomes may be crucial for the individual.

Manufacturers have serious problems with machine set-up time. For example, in one company, set-up time was sufficiently excessive that Wittkopp, Rowan, and Poling (1991) increased gross profit of the machines by an estimated 10.4%, using a behavioral intervention that reduced set-up time. I suggest that set-up time is so great because of the problem of small and cumulating outcomes. Each single instance of being off task (e.g., taking an unscheduled coffee break) during set-up has a minimal aversive impact (e.g., decreased gross profit). Only the cumulative effect of many such instances is significant. And each single instance of especially efficient behavior (e.g., cleaning the press properly before beginning set-up) has a minimal positive impact (e.g., increased gross profit). Again, only the cumulative effect of many such instances is significant. (In some instances the cumulative effect may be significant only for the organization; however, in some instances the cumulative effect of poor or good performance may also be significant for the individual in terms of praise, a raise, a promotion, or gain sharing [Gowen, 1989; Mawhinney & Gowen, 1989].)

But those harmful effects accumulate into a significant outcome only after a considerable delay. So perhaps the delay is why the operators are too often off task and too often inefficient when on task, in spite of the costly results. In other words, there are two "psychological" reasons the harmful outcomes of being off task are not part of a direct-acting contingency that punishes that behavior: (1) The immediate, harmful outcomes are too small. (2) The sizeable harmful outcomes are too delayed. (Of course, also there can be a "physical" reason: Workers may never even learn of the cumulated harmful outcomes of their poor performances.) But the question here is not why the outcomes are not part of a direct-acting punishment contingency. The question is: Why are rules describing such contingencies so hard to follow? (A parallel analysis applies to the benefits of being on task.)

To answer that question, consider the following hypothetical rule: "A single unauthorized coffee break will reduce your machine's gross profit by 10.4% for the year; however, that decrease will not take effect until exactly one year after the illegal coffee break." Any operator who was planning to stay with the company for the next year, should have no problem complying with such an easy-to-follow rule, though the outcome would be delayed. This suggests that, rather than the delay, it is the small and cumulative nature of the natural contingency that makes the real rule so hard to follow. (While emphasizing the delay, Brown and Herrnstein [1975, p. 188], also point to the problem of the small but cumulative contingency.)

IMPROBABLE OUTCOMES

Contingencies with improbable outcomes also cause serious problems, because they too often fail to control behavior, even when rules describe them. For example, consider occupational safety: As Sulzer-Azaroff, Loafman, Merante, and Hlavacek (1990) point out, the probability of accidents are low, in spite of unsafe practices and in spite of the lack of safe practices. Probably the worker will be OK, in any specific instance, though he or she acts unsafely by wearing shoes without closed toes and heels, by lifting more than a standard load, and by leaving carts outside designated areas. And probably the worker will be OK, in any specific instance, though he or she fails to wear eye protection, label containers, and mop up wet spots. Rules describing these natural contingencies are hard to follow because they describe low probability outcomes, even though, with enough workers doing enough unsafe acts, the absolute numbers of accidents and injuries can sometimes be high and costly for both workers and management.

Ineffective Contingencies and Self-Management

I suggest that people tend to follow rules describing indirect-acting contingencies, though the outcomes are delayed, as long as those outcomes are sizeable and probable. For example, in a public utility, Smith, Kaminski, and Wylie (1990) found that employees submitted 89 suggestions in a 9 month period. The employees made these suggestions, though the outcomes were delayed: The management would not give initial monetary awards for the suggestions until the reviewers had an opportunity to evaluate the suggestions; and management would not give a supplemental monetary award until they had calculated the actual savings the suggestions had generated over a 2 year period. According to the present rule-governed analysis, the rule describing the contingencies for making suggestions controlled the employees' behavior because it described outcomes that were sizeable and probable: The median initial award was $275, and the maximum possible supplemental award was $50,000; also the probability of an award was fairly high, 0.13.

However people tend not to follow rules that specify contingencies with small but cumulative outcomes and improbable (though immediate) outcomes. (Therefore, such contingencies are *ineffective contingencies*.) For example, Henry and Redmon (1990) found that machine operators did not reliably analyze the summary data needed for statistical process control (SPC). One interpretation is that workers failed to do so because of the size, complexity, and abstract nature of the tasks and because the tasks "seem so removed from the actual product." However, the present analysis suggests that workers did not reliably do SPC because the outcome (improved quality) was too small to support each individual SPC act. Henry and Redmon's data agree with this rule-governed analysis. They increased the median percentage of SPC acts from 78% to 100% by changing from a rule that specified a small but cumulatively sizeable outcome to one that specified a moderately sizeable outcome. They changed the implicit rule from, "each SPC act will produce a small and only cumulatively significant improvement in quality," to "each SPC act will affect the daily (though delayed) feedback the quality-control manager gives you," (a more sizeable outcome).

We can summarize this section as follows: Rules are easy to follow, if they describe outcomes that are both sizeable and probable. The delay is not crucial. Rules are hard to follow, if they describe outcomes that are either too small (though often of cumulative significance) or too improbable. The delay is not crucial.

Figure 1 shows two types of rules easy to follow and hard to follow. Rules that are easy to follow describe two types of contingencies: direct-acting and indirect-acting contingencies. For a contingency to be direct acting, the outcome must be all three: immediate, probable, and sizeable. For a contingency to be indirect acting, the outcome must be delayed, probable, and sizeable (if the outcome were not delayed, the contingency would be direct acting). Rules that are hard to follow describe ineffective contingencies. For a contingency to be ineffective (for verbal human beings), the outcome must be either improbable or small, regardless of whether it is immediate or delayed.

PERFORMANCE MANAGEMENT

To lead into a discussion of the relation between rule-governed behavior and performance management, let me raise three questions:

1. When do we need performance management? We need performance management when the contingencies normally present are

ineffective in supporting appropriate behavior. By *appropriate behavior* I mean behavior that does two things: (a) It increases the individual's and the group's long-range contact with beneficial conditions; (b) It also decreases contact with harmful conditions. (Often, though far from always, *beneficial conditions* means *reinforcers* and *harmful conditions* means *aversive conditions.* However, we might best minimize overall contact with aversive conditions by using performance-management contingencies that are made maximally effective because of an underlying component of aversive control.)

2. How do we manage the performance of nonverbal clients? We add or remove effective direct-acting contingencies of reinforcement and punishment, to supplement the ineffective normal contingencies (e.g., Blount, Drabman, Wilson, and Stewart, 1982).

The answer to this third question, suggests the relevance to organizational behavior management of a theory of rule-governed behavior:

3. How do we manage the performance of verbal clients? Instead of adding direct-acting contingencies, we often add indirect-acting contingencies to the ineffective natural contingencies. In other words, we supplement rules that are hard to follow by adding rules that are easy to follow. (Of course, sometimes we also add or remove direct-acting contingencies.)

For example, consider a university admissions department with a serious backlog of applications for admission. Each application processor completed a median of only 30 daily tasks. After an intervention by Wilk and Redmon (1990), the number of tasks completed daily rose to 99. Wilk and Redmon did this by changing from a rule that specified a small though cumulatively sizeable outcome to rules that specified moderately sizeable outcomes, though those outcomes were delayed.

Originally this rule described the existing contingency:

"Completing each processing task will produce a small and only cumulatively significant decrease in the backlog of admissions applications." This natural contingency was ineffective in supporting a high enough rate of task completion because the outcome was too small and of only cumulative significance.

The following rule described the contingencies Wilk and Redmon set up: "Completing each processing task assigned today will determine the

FIGURE 1. A taxonomy of rules.

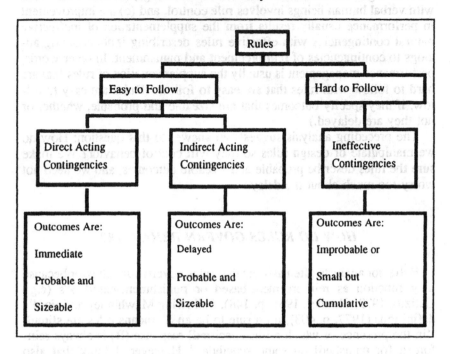

feedback your supervisor gives you tomorrow morning.'' This rule described an effective indirect-acting rule-governed analog to what was probably a combination of reinforcement and avoidance contingencies. The analog to reinforcement involved the supervisor's praise, and the analog to avoidance involved the aversiveness of confronting the failure of not having met the previous day's goal. These are analog contingencies and do not directly reinforce the completion of tasks, because the delivery of the outcomes does not occur until the next day. Thus the processor's behavior must have been under the control of the rules describing those contingencies rather than directly under the control of the contingencies themselves (i.e., those contingencies were indirect acting). (Incidentally, in their intervention package, Wilk and Redmon also added two direct-acting contingencies; twice daily, the supervisor praised each application processor who was on task at the moment and gave corrective feedback to each processor who was off task.)

This example illustrates the notions that (a) most performance management in organizations involves verbal human beings, (b) most such work with verbal human beings involves rule control, and (c) the improvement in performance usually results from the supplementation of ineffective natural contingencies with effective rules describing indirect-acting analogs to contingencies of reinforcement and punishment. In other words, performance management is usually the supplementation of rules that are hard to follow with rules that are easy to follow. (Rules are easy to follow, if they specify outcomes that are sizeable and probable, whether or not they are delayed.)

The preceding analysis suggests an answer to this question: How do we manipulate or design rules so they will control behavior? We make sure the rules describe probable and sizeable outcomes, and we need not worry too much about the delay.

HOW DO RULES GOVERN BEHAVIOR?

Behavior analysts often assume that rules govern our behavior because they function as reinforcement-based or punishment-based S^Ds (e.g., Galizio, 1979; Skinner, 1966, p. 148). Following Mawhinney and Ford's definitions (1977, p. 403), for a rule to be an S^D means rules are stimuli "in the presence of which a [the specified] response (R) is always reinforced [or punished] on some schedule." However, I think that also should mean the absence of the rule is a reinforcement-based or punishment-based Ess Delta—"a stimulus in the presence of which a response is never [or is less likely] to be reinforced [or punished]." But rules might not always work that way.

Consider the problem of procrastination: A person has four hours to finish a project before the deadline. The person states this rule: "If I do not get to work right now, I will miss the deadline and look bad." The rule describes an indirect-acting analog to an avoidance contingency.

Because this analog contingency is in effect regardless of the rule statement, perhaps the rule does not function as an analog to an S^D nor its absence as an analog to an Ess Delta. Instead, the rule statement might function as a conditioned establishing operation (Michael, 1982) that establishes noncompliance with the rule as a learned aversive condition. (Some would call that aversive condition fear, or guilt, or anxiety, or nervousness.)

So, stating the rule about starting to prepare might be an establishing operation, like turning on the shock in an escape experiment (or more precisely, like a learned establishing operation like turning on the warning stimulus in and avoidance experiment). And making the last-minute preparations is the escape response that attenuates the learned aversive condition. Perhaps, merely starting to work reduces the aversiveness a bit; and finishing the task may allow the person to completely escape this self-generated aversive condition.

However, sometimes rules might also function as S^Ds, because sometimes they are stimuli "in the presence of which a (the specified) response (R) is always reinforced [or punished] on some schedule." Cerutti (1989, p. 261) gives an example: "A child's turning can be reinforced given the vocal stimulus 'turn,' jumping can be reinforced given 'jump.'" Of course the mere statement of a rule will not control behavior. The rule must be credible. In other words, it should not contradict more credible rules nor obvious experience (Galizio, 1979; Mawhinney & Ford, 1977, p. 409; Rao & Mawhinney, 1991), for example rules based on direct contact with contingencies. And it should come from a credible source—a source similar to sources of reliable rules in the past. All of this depends on an appropriate behavioral history, as does the credibility of the source of rules specifying outcomes in an afterlife.

Note that this overall analysis suggests direct-acting escape contingencies control our rule-governed behavior, even when the rule describes an indirect-acting contingency. For example, working to avoid looking bad as a consequence of failing to meet the deadline involves an indirect-acting contingency, because the outcome is delayed from the behavior of finishing the preparations; and the delay means the outcome is not part of a direct-acting avoidance contingency that would reinforce those final preparations. But all operant control may require direct-acting contingencies; so I have theorized that the most likely direct-acting contingency is an escape contingency based on the learned aversive condition resulting from stating the rule combined with noncompliance. (For an alternative analysis, see Schlinger and Blakely, 1987.)

We can ask, what causes these rules to be stated? Someone else might state the rule specifying the deadline, for example a nagging spouse, parent, teacher, or employer. Or no one might state the rule, and thus the person would fail to meet the deadline. Casual observation suggests this happens fairly often; and that makes theoretical sense, because stating deadline rules should generate an aversive condition that would tend to punish the statement of that rule. The punishment contingency would suppress the rule statement unless stronger reinforcement, escape, or avoidance contingencies countervail. Such stronger countervailing contingencies must be the result of elaborate and complex behavioral histories. A simple example might involve the prompting parent who would frequently ask with a sarcastic tone, "Don't you have something you should be doing now?"

An example of a variation might be as follows: Finding yourself unproductively engaged during the working hours is a learned aversive condition. You escape that aversive condition by asking yourself what you need to do, stating the appropriate rule and starting to work. If you start to work soon enough, the level of aversiveness you are escaping may be so low as to be unnoticed, even though it controls your behavior.

Consistent with the preceding emphasis on aversive control, I have argued elsewhere (Malott, 1990) that we may not be able to build a world free of aversive control. A major reason is that much of our behavior needs to be under the control of contingencies involving deadlines; and failure to complete the relevant task before the deadline will result in the presentation of an aversive condition or the loss of either a current reinforcer or the opportunity to receive a reinforcer. In other words, deadlines always seem to involve aversive control, as is suggested by the frequent complaints people make about deadlines. (Here, I am referring to the aversiveness associated with failure to meet a deadline. Optimal duration theory may suggest an additional source of aversiveness associated with deadlines, in that "to the extent that one is forced to engage in an activity for a longer duration than one's optimal duration or to be exposed to the optimal duration more frequently than one's preferred interval would permit, the event will be aversive" [Mawhinney, 1979].)

Larger unlearned reinforcers is not a way out of the pervasive (though often low-level) aversiveness of our world, unless we are more deprived of those reinforcers than most of us would care to be. Adding larger learned generalized reinforcers such as money does not prevent our procrastinating until we are aversively close to the deadline. And it does not seem technically feasible to increase the intrinsic reinforcers in all of our tasks to the point where we do not need deadlines.

Incidentally, we might ask how a particular rule enters a person's repertoire. Perhaps the most common way is that someone else tells the person the rule; that someone could be, for example, a supervisor, a parent, a teacher, or a friend. Or the person might infer the rule, either from contact with the indirect-acting contingency or from an analysis of the potential contingencies prior to making contact with that contingency.

RULE-GOVERNED BEHAVIOR, BEHAVIORAL ANTHROPOLOGY, AND ORGANIZATIONAL CULTURE

In the preceding sections, we have considered a theory of rule-governed behavior as it applies to organizational behavior. This theory also applies to an overall view of culture in general and organizational culture in particular.

The anthropologist Marvin Harris (1974) presented a compelling argument that materialistic contingencies control practices of cultures in general. He further argued that those practices do so because they maximize the materialistic benefits to the members of that culture. For instance, the Indian farmer tends the sacred cow, because of the tending's materialistic benefits (milk, fertilizer, fuel, offspring, and plowed fields). In the same way, the farmer does not slaughter that sacred cow, because of the loss of those future benefits (the loss would have a terrible impact on the fragile economy of most Indian farmers).

Harris treated such materialistic contingencies as if they were direct-acting contingencies of reinforcement and punishment. Therefore, in his battle against mentalistic anthropology, Harris analyzed the evolution and maintenance of cultural practices as if simple materialistic contingencies of reinforcement and punishment were responsible.

On the other hand, such materialistic contingencies might not usually be direct acting, because their outcomes were too delayed, too improbable, or of only small and cumulative value (Malott, 1988). For example, a single instance of tending the cow produces too small an increment in the farmer's materialistic benefits to reinforce that tending; also those materialistic benefits are too delayed. So these materialistic contingencies must be indirect-acting analogs to reinforcement and punishment contingencies, to the extent that they control behavior. This, in turn, means rule-governed behavior must be involved. (See Glenn, 1989, for another analysis of the role of verbal behavior in supporting cultural practices. Also see Brown and Herrnstein, 1975, p. 166-167, for a cultural-materialistic analysis of the behavior of the New Guinea wild-pig hunters. These hunters gave their catch to the community, instead of eating it themselves. Like Harris, Brown and Herrnstein also treat these materialistic contingencies as if they were direct acting, though they are often delayed, and probably small and cumulative.)

However, much of the rule-governed behavior may be by cultural planners, designers, managers, or leaders; these people must be able to state rules describing those materialistic contingencies. In other words, for cultural practices to deal effectively with contingencies that are not direct acting, at least the leaders must be able to describe those contingencies. Scott and Podsakoff (1985, p. 177-193) make a similar point about organizational culture:

> If an organization is to thrive and survive, it must be structured so the behavior of the members continues to satisfy the reinforcement contingencies prevailing in the external environment. However, the external contingencies are sometimes dynamic as well as complex. Therefore, some organizational members, including most certainly the leader of leaders, will be required to monitor the environment for "opportunities" and "threats," to consider alternative modes of organizational adjustment, and to propose or implement such modifications in organizational structure as are required by the changes in the external environment or achieve a combination of these. . . . It is clear that leaders of leaders must be capable of analyzing, designing, and modifying organizational structure. . . . We, of course, take the position that the human organism is perfectly capable of analyzing complex contingencies and maximizing reinforcing consequences.

Along the same lines, Mawhinney (1982) empirically demonstrated that "people may develop formal analyses of reinforcement contingencies such as concurrent schedules, and extract rules for maximization of reinforcements from them which override any innate propensity to match" (p. 280). Mawhinney then points out that this sort of control by rules is "what Skinner (1969) calls 'rule governed behavior' " (p. 280).

Although Scott and Podsakoff do not distinguish between direct and indirect-acting contingencies, they seem to imply that leaders of organizations must be able to state rules describing those contingencies, just as I am suggesting that leaders of cultures must. Also, they criticize Skinner's (1971, Chapter 10) analysis of the evolution of cultures (and implicitly organizations), when he suggests that the processes are parallel to the evolution of a species through the contingencies of natural selection. This seems similar to my critique of Harris's analysis. Both Harris and Skinner appear to have ignored the important role of leaders who can describe the relevant external contingencies and prescribe cultural or organizational rules for practices that will effectively cope with those contingencies (of course, when the leaders err, so much the worse for that culture).

Scott and Podsakoff also define organizational structure (and perhaps implicitly organizational culture) as "the set of social reinforcement contingencies that prevail in every organization and that 'serve to shape and channel' the behavior of its participants" (p. 179). (By social reinforcement contingencies, they mean the delivery of any sort of reinforcers mediated by another person [See Rao and Mawhinney, 1991, for an experimental analysis of such organizational social-reinforcement contingencies].)

The emphasis of the present paper is on that part of the organizational culture (the delivery of reinforcers and aversive conditions mediated by another person) involving indirect-acting contingencies, because indirect-acting contingencies are those with which organizational behavior management has primarily dealt. And because those contingencies are indirect acting, we must deal with the role of rules in the control these organizational-cultural contingencies exert over the behavior of the members of organizations.

OTHER CONCERNS

The present article mainly deals with the control by rules describing indirect-acting contingencies. Therefore, it is interpretative, because most of the experimental work deals with rules describing direct-acting contingencies (e.g., Matthews, Catania, & Shimoff, 1985; for experimental work with indirect-acting contingencies, see Braam and Malott, 1991).

Behavioral Units

One issue is the size and complexity of the behavioral unit controlled by rule statements. Mawhinney and Ford (1977) point out that stimulus-response chains comprised of sequences of responses terminating in a reinforcer can vary considerably in their size and complexity. They further point to Zeiler's (1970) work with pigeons involving direct-acting contingencies of reinforcement on a fixed-ratio schedule where the time the pigeon used to complete a ratio of key pecks varied as a function of the time available (limited hold or deadline). Such homogeneous stimulus-response chains can be, as Zeiler says, "treated as individual responses and . . . reinforced according to some schedule." Similarly Cerutti (1989, p. 263) suggests that, after being described in a rule, "complex [homogeneous or heterogeneous] responses may retain their integrity over time and situations."

So direct-acting contingencies can reinforce (and no doubt punish) a molar response consisting of a sequence of component responses. Such experimental data combine with our everyday experience and common sense to suggest that rules can describe this sort of direct-acting contingency and can also control molar responses, not just small individual responses. How does this apply to the size of behavioral units controlled by rules describing indirect-acting contingencies?

To answer this, we should consider the concept of *analogs to stimulus-response chains*. An *analog chain* is one where an intermediate or terminal outcome is too delayed to reinforce or punish the preceding behavior or where an initial or intermediate antecedent stimulus is too delayed from the opportunity to respond "appropriately" for that stimulus to function as an S^D. (For example, suppose you put a pigeon in a test chamber and flashed a green light for a fraction of a second. Then a week later you gave the pigeon the opportunity to make a reinforced response. And when the light was red, the delayed response would not be reinforced. It seems unlikely that the light color would come to exert stimulus control over the delayed key peck. We would not call the green light an S^D because the opportunity for a reinforced response was too delayed. It is not a stimulus in the presence of which the response was reinforced.)

However, with a similar set of temporal parameters, the light could exert stimulus control over the delayed but reinforced key peck of a verbal human being. But the mere fact of stimulus control should not cause us to classify the light as an S^D because, as the pigeon demonstrated, the green light was not paired in sufficient proximity with reinforcement. Instead, for the verbal human being, this historical stimulus might better be considered an *analog to an S^D*. And so such linked sequences of stimuli and responses might better be considered *analogs to stimulus-response chains* whenever they involve analog S^Ds or delayed reinforcers. Furthermore, we would expect that rules describing these analogs to stimulus-response chains could control the behavior of verbal human beings. Therefore, rules should be able to control behavior when they describe molar responses involved in contingencies with large, complex analogs to stimulus-response chains, not just when they describe simple responses. So there can be a wide range in the size and complexity of the behavioral unit controlled by rules describing indirect-acting contingencies.

Individual Differences in Rule Control

People vary greatly in their professional and personal success. Much of this difference seems to be a function of their success at managing their own behavior (self-management, time management). In turn, their success at managing their own behavior is a function of the extent to which their behavioral histories have established the needed repertoires. I suggest people's success at self-management is a function of the extent to which their behavior is under the control of rules describing contingencies that are not direct acting. The individual differences in such rule control would seem to be a function of behavioral history. For example, following from the earlier analysis of procrastination, there seems to be a great difference among people in terms of how close they must get to the deadline before not working to meet the deadline becomes so aversive that they escape or attenuate that aversiveness by starting to work. This temporal gradient of aversiveness seems likely to be a function of behavioral history. Pity the person whose behavioral history has not established failure to begin work as sufficiently aversive to reinforce the appropriate escape response. Such people seem to exist, at least to some extent (and at least to some extent, in most of us). Elsewhere (Malott, 1989), I discuss other prerequisites for control by rules specifying contingencies that are not direct acting (and implicitly sources of individual differences), all of which are a function of the person's behavioral history.

None of this is to suggest that the person is to be held responsible for the behavioral history that generated or failed to generate an effective self-management repertoire. However, as professional behavior analysts working with organizations, it is our responsibility to help the person either acquire an effective self-management repertoire or to provide a set of supplemental performance-management contingencies described by rules that are easy to follow and that will allow such a person to perform both to the satisfaction of himself or herself and to the satisfaction of his or her employees. We seem much more successful at performance management with supplemental rules than at improving the self-management skills of adults (for an analysis of rule-governed behavior and self-management, see Malott, 1986).

CONCLUSIONS

This paper has presented an analysis of organizational culture in terms of rule-governed behavior. The following are the implications:

> Many of the contingencies that define an organization's culture are indirect acting, because their outcomes are too delayed to reinforce or punish the causal behavior.

Rules describing these cultural contingencies allow them to indirectly control behavior.

Such rules fail to govern behavior when they describe ineffective contingencies involving outcomes that are either too improbable or too small and of only cumulative significance, despite their delay. These rules are hard to follow.

The delay between the behavior and the outcome is crucial for contingencies of reinforcement but has little effect when rules describe those contingencies.

Performance management consists of adding rules that are easy to follow–rules describing contingencies with outcomes that are both probable and sizeable, regardless of their delay.

The present theoretical analysis suggests that rules describing such indirect-acting contingencies are easy to follow because they act as establishing operations that establish noncompliance as an effectively aversive motivating condition–one that will support direct-acting escape and punishment contingencies. In other words, delayed, indirect-acting contingencies, by themselves will not control behavior.

Because of the prevalence of indirect-acting contingencies, we cannot adequately analyze the contingencies of an organization's culture (e.g., gainsharing), without reference to rule-governed behavior.

(For a more detailed treatment of this theory of rule-governed behavior, including considerations of alternative analyses, compatibility with such phenomena as delayed taste aversion, and the behavioral prerequisites needed for rules to govern behavior, see Malott, 1989.)

REFERENCES

Ainslie, G. (1975). Specious reward: A behavioral theory of impulsiveness and impulse control. *Psychological Bulletin, 28*, 463-496.

Blount, R. L., Drabman, R. S., Wilson, N., & Stewart, D. (1982). Reducing severe diurnal bruxism in two profoundly retarded females. *Journal of Applied Behavior Analysis, 15*, 565-571.

Braam, C., & Malott, R. W. (1991). "I'll do it when the snow melts." The effects of deadlines and delays on rule-governed behavior. *The Analysis of Verbal Behavior, 8*, 67-76.

Brown, M. G., Malott, R. W., Dillon, M. J., & Keeps, E. J. (1980). Improving customer service in a large department store through the use of training and feedback. *Journal of Organizational Behavior Management, 2,* 251-266.

Brown, R., & Herrnstein, R. J. (1975). *Psychology.* Boston: Little, Brown, and Company.

Cerutti, D. T. (1989). Discrimination theory of rule-governed behavior. *Journal of the Experimental Analysis of Behavior, 51,* 259-276.

Chung, S. H., & Herrnstein, R. J. (1967). Choice and delay of reinforcement. *Journal of the Experimental Analysis of Behavior, 10,* 67-74.

Chung, S. H. (1965). Effects of delayed reinforcement in a concurrent choice situation. *Journal of the Experimental Analysis of Behavior, 8,* 439-444.

Galizio, M. (1979). Contingency-shaped and rule-governed behavior: Instructional control of human loss avoidance. *Journal of the Experimental Analysis of Behavior, 31,* 53-70.

Glenn, S. S. (1989). Verbal behavior and cultural practices. *Behavior Analysis and Social Action, 7,* 10-15.

Gowen, C. R., III (1990). Gainsharing programs: An overview of history and research. *Journal of Organizational Behavior Management, 11* (2), 77-99.

Harris, M. (1974). *Cows, pigs, wars and witches: The riddles of culture.* New York: Random House.

Henry, G. O., & Redmon, W. K. (1990). The effects of performance feedback on the implementation of a statistical process control (SPC) program. *Journal of Organizational Behavior Management, 11* (2), 23-46.

Lett, B. T. (1973). Delayed reward learning: Disproof of the traditional theory. *Learning and Motivation, 4,* 237-246.

Logue, A. W., Peña-Correal, T. E., Rodriguez, M. L., & Kabela, E. (1986). Self-control in adult humans: Variation in positive reinforcer amount and delay. *Journal of the Experimental Analysis of Behavior, 46,* 159-173.

Malott, R. W., & Malott, M. E. (1991). Private events and rule-governed behavior. In L. J. Hayes & P. N. Chase (Eds.) *Dialogues on verbal behavior.* (pp. 237-254). Reno, NV: Context Press.

Malott, R. W., Shimamune, S., & Malott, M. E. (1992). Rule-governed behavior and organization behavior management: An analyses of the literature. *Journal of Organizational Behavior Management, 12,* (2).

Malott, R. W. (1986). Self-management, rule-governed behavior, and everyday life. In H. W. Reese & L. J. Parrott (Eds.), *Behavioral science: Philosophical, methodological, and empirical advances,* Hillsdale, NJ: Lawrence Erlbaum Associates, 207-228.

Malott, R. W. (1988). Rule-governed behavior and behavioral anthropology. *The Behavior Analyst, 11,* 181-203.

Malott, R. W. (1989). The achievement of evasive goals: Control by rules describing indirect-acting contingencies. In S. C. Hayes (Ed.), *Rule-governed behavior: Cognition, contingencies, and instructional control* (pp. 269-322). New York: Plenum.

Malott, R. W. (1990, Fall). Notes from a radical behaviorist: Can we build a world free of aversive control? *The ABA Newsletter, 13,* 10.

Matthews, B. A., Catania, A. C., & Shimoff, E. (1985). Effects of uninstructed verbal behavior on nonverbal responding: Contingency descriptions versus performance descriptions. *Journal of the Experimental Analysis of Behavior, 43,* 155-164.

Mawhinney, T. C. (1975). Operant terms and concepts in the description of individual work behavior: Some problems of interpretation, application, and evaluation. *Journal of Applied Psychology, 60,* 704-712.

Mawhinney, T. C. (1979). Intrinsic X extrinsic work motivation: Perspectives from behaviorism. *Organizational Behavior and Human Performance, 24,* 411-440.

Mawhinney, T. C. (1982). Maximizing versus matching in people versus pigeons. *Psychological Reports, 50,* 267-281.

Mawhinney, T. C., & Ford, J. D. (1977). The path goal theory of leader effectiveness: An operant interpretation. *Academy of Management Review, 2,* 398-411.

Mawhinney, T. C., & Gowen, C. R., III (1990). Gainsharing and the law of effect as the matching law: A theoretical framework. *Journal of Organizational Behavior Management, 11* (2), 61-75.

Michael, J. L. (1982). Distinguishing between discriminative and motivational functions of stimuli. *Journal of the Experimental Analysis of Behavior, 37,* 149-155.

Rachlin, H., & Green, L. (1972). Commitment, choice and self-control. *Journal of Experimental Analysis of Behavior, 17,* 15-22.

Rao, R. K. & Mawhinney, T. C. (1991). Superior-Subordinate dyads: Dependence of Leader effectiveness on Mutual Reinforcement Contingencies. *Journal of Experimental Analysis of Behavior, 56,* 105-118.

Schlinger, H., & Blakely, E. (1987). Function-altering effects of contingency-specifying stimuli. *The Behavior Analyst, 10,* 41-45.

Scott, W. E., & Podsakoff, P. M. (1985). *Behavioral principles in the practice of management.* New York: John Wiley & Sons.

Shimp, C. P. (1969). The concurrent reinforcement of two interresponse times: The relative harmonic length. *Journal of the Experimental Analysis of Behavior, 12,* 402-411.

Skinner, B. F. (1969). *Contingencies of reinforcement: A theoretical analysis.* New York: Appleton-Century Crofts.

Skinner, B. F. (1971). *Beyond freedom and dignity.* New York: Knopf.

Smith, J. M., Kaminski, B. J., & Wylie, R. G. (1990). May I make a suggestion?: Corporate support for innovation. *Journal of Organizational Behavior Management, 11* (2), 125-146.

Sulzer-Azaroff, B., Loafman, B., Merante, R. J., & Hlavacek, A. C. (1990). Improving occupational safety in a large industrial plant: A systematic replication. *Journal of Organizational Behavior Management, 11* (2), 99-120.

Weisberg, P., & Waldrop, P. B. (1972). Fixed-interval work habits of congress. *Journal of Applied Behavior Analysis, 5,* 93-97.

Wilk, L. A., & Redmon, W. K. (1990). A daily-adjusted goal-setting and feedback procedure for improving productivity in a university admissions department. *Journal of Organizational Behavior Management, 11* (2), 55-75.

Wittkopp, C. J., Rowan, J. F., & Poling, A. (1990). Use of a feedback package to reduce machine set-up time in a manufacturing setting. *Journal of Organizational Behavior Management, 11* (1), 7-22.

Zeiler, M . D. (1970). Time limits for completing fixed ratios. *Journal of the Experimental Analysis of Behavior, 14*, 275-286.

Contingency Specifying Stimuli: The Role of "Rules" in Organizational Behavior Management

Judy L. Agnew
William K. Redmon

Frequently, reports of Organizational Behavior Management (OBM) research describe procedures (e.g., feedback, goal setting), but fail to identify the behavioral mechanisms which underlie those procedures (Duncan & Bruwelheide, 1986). Furthermore, when behavioral explanations are provided, they are couched too often in terms of simple antecedents and consequences which fail to represent accurately the complex contingencies that operate outside the laboratory. If a better understanding of organizational behavior is to be achieved, more comprehensive analyses must be conducted and reported (Duncan & Bruwelheide, 1986; Mawhinney, 1975; Peterson, 1982). In many cases this means that OBM researchers and practitioners must adopt more complex behavioral concepts. Contingency specifying stimuli, or "rules" represent one such concept and are the subject of this paper.

A FUNCTIONAL DEFINITION OF "RULES"

"Rules" are verbal stimuli that *describe* behavioral contingencies, in Skinner's (1969) words, "contingency specifying stimuli." These verbal stimuli are expressed in frames of the form "if . . . then . . ." (Vaughan, 1989). For example, one might state the following rule: "If I arrive at work on time, I will receive points worth money." This statement specifies a behavior and a consequence and relates them in an "if . . . then"

Judy L. Agnew is currently a consultant with Aubrey Daniels and Associates, Inc., Tucker, GA. William K. Redmon is affiliated with the Department of Psychology, Western Michigan University.

Requests for reprints may be sent to William K. Redmon at: Department of Psychology, Western Michigan University, Kalamazoo, MI 49008-5052.

frame. A rule also may specify conditions under which a behavior should occur. For example consider the following statement: "If I arrive at work on time on Monday morning, I will receive points worth money." In this version of a rule, behavior must be emitted under specific conditions (i.e., Monday morning) in order for the consequences (i.e., points) to be delivered.

Some have suggested that rules function as discriminative stimuli (S^Ds) that describe a contingency and evoke the behavior described by the contingency (e.g., Brownstein & Shull, 1985; Huber, 1986; Skinner, 1969). However, others have argued that control over behavior by rules is more complex (Cerutti, 1989; Schlinger & Blakely, 1987). Schlinger and Blakely (1987) argued convincingly against the classification of rules as S^Ds and provided a potentially useful alternative definition. It is this definition that will be adopted in this paper and suggested for use in OBM research and practice. Schlinger and Blakely (1987) point out that rules do not fit the definition of a discriminative stimulus in that all rules do not evoke behavior (i.e., immediately strengthen behavior). For example, the rule, "If I hand in my report by five p.m. on Friday, I can go home for the weekend" does not immediately evoke the behavior of handing in the report. Rather, it affects the probability of handing in the report at 5 p.m. on Friday. That is, in the future, when the correct time and day are noted, the behavior of handing in the report should be more likely to occur. The rule becomes part of the contingency in that if the rule had not been stated, the day and time might not have evoked the behavior. Thus, Schlinger and Blakely argue that rules should not be classified as discriminative stimuli, but as "function-altering" stimuli.

According to this position, rules influence behavior by changing the function of other stimuli; and it is those other stimuli, whose function has been altered, that directly control the behavior. These authors elaborate by examining how rules can alter not just the evocative function of discriminative stimuli, but also the reinforcing or punishing functions of consequent stimuli, and the function of stimuli in respondent (classical conditioning) relations. In addition, Schlinger and Blakely point out that a rule may have many function-altering effects simultaneously. To return to the example of handing in a report, the rule might alter the function of the day and time in more than one way. Following statement of the rule, the time of day might serve as an S^D which increases the probability of handing in a report and, at the same time, as a conditioned stimulus which produces physical responses that we might label "anxiety" or "stress."

In a second paper, Blakely and Schlinger (1987) supplemented their initial assertion, about the inaccuracy of classifying rules as S^Ds, by pointing out that doing so obscures the function-altering effects of rules. Thus, to inaccurately call a rule an S^D, results in an inaccurate explanation of the functional effects of that rule. Therefore, they propose that "rules" be defined as function-altering, contingency-specifying stimuli and that the term be used exclusively for such stimuli. They note that some verbal stimuli actually function as S^Ds; for example, the phrase "put that down" could accurately be classified as an S^D in that it functions to immediately evoke behavior, if it does evoke the behavior. Such statements, however, do not fit the classification of a contingency-specifying stimulus (i.e., do not describe a complete contingency) and, thus, should not be called a "rule."

RULE CONTROL: AN ILLUSTRATION

An example of the possible effect of rules on behavior is provided by research on humans responding under various schedules of reinforcement. Prior to empirical investigations, it was predicted that verbal humans exposed to the various schedules of reinforcement would demonstrate the same steady states of behavior displayed by nonhuman laboratory animals under these schedules (e.g., a scalloped pattern characteristic of fixed interval schedule control). Empirical research has not always supported these predictions. Although nonverbal humans demonstrate responding similar to that of other animals, the response patterns of verbal humans have been shown to differ significantly from patterns produced by nonhuman subjects (e.g., Bentall, Lowe & Beasty, 1985; Leander, Lippman & Meyer, 1968). This research suggests that humans may develop rules about the contingencies of reinforcement to which they are exposed and behave in accordance with their self-stated rules, regardless of the planned contingencies.[1] Such effects may be the result of rules stated by subjects in response to the contingencies of an experiment or management program. As Vaughan (1989) suggests, "self-talk may underlie and influence much of human adult responding" (p. 110). She adds that self-talk "at least sometimes determine[s] the form of the response as well as its probability of occurrence," and that "we can no longer ignore this additional controlling variable" (p. 110).

RULES AND PERFORMANCE FEEDBACK

To illustrate how rules might be functioning in an organizational intervention, an example using performance feedback (PF) will be described.

PF is the most common type of OBM intervention; in fact, some form of PF was used in over half of the interventions reported in the first five volumes of the *Journal of Organizational Behavior Management* (Balcazar, Hopkins & Suarez, 1986).

Feedback stimuli are usually categorized as discriminative stimuli or reinforcers (Peterson, 1982); however, an analysis of feedback interventions with reference to the precise definitions of discriminative stimulus and reinforcing stimulus leads to a rejection of these simple classifications. If feedback functioned as an S^D, it would have to be correlated consistently with the presentation of a reinforcer and would have to evoke behavior immediately. If feedback functioned as a reinforcer or punisher, it would have to follow behavior immediately and increase the probability of the behavior in the immediate future. These relations are observed only rarely in organizational settings.

Although feedback does not fit the strict definition of either reinforcer or discriminative stimulus, its use often results in behavior change. In the absence of additional, observable contingencies which might support the behavior, it is possible that rule effects are involved. In Peterson's (1982) words, "It is probably the case that many examples of feedback, especially when provided on an infrequent basis, can be explained in terms of rule-governed behavior . . ." (p. 102).

Assume that a worker receives feedback on past performance, such as a graph depicting performance trends, without accompanying stimuli (e.g., no verbal explanations of the purpose of the feedback, no additional reinforcing or punishing stimuli). The worker might develop a rule such as, "if I perform well my hard work will show on the feedback graph, and my supervisor may decide to give me a raise," or, "if I don't perform well the feedback graph will look bad and I may be fired." Despite formal differences, both rules could alter the function of stimuli associated with working harder (e.g., evidence of work to be completed could become a discriminative stimulus which affects the amount of work done, and evidence of work completed could become a reinforcing stimulus); and, after the statement of the rule, such stimuli might come to maintain the behavior of working harder.

The source of rules is an issue worthy of consideration. Rules may be provided by management or co-workers in organizational settings (e.g., a supervisor may explicitly state a rule to an employee), or workers may develop their own rules to describe contingencies they can identify readily. When left to develop their own rules, workers may or may not create rules that support appropriate behavior. For example, a worker may state a rule such as: "if I work harder and my supervisor notices, she'll just raise the performance standards, and I'll end up having to work harder and harder for the same money." Regardless of the accuracy of the statement, this rule is likely to lead to the maintenance of current levels of performance, or perhaps, a reduction in performance. Such rules would explain reports that the effectiveness of feedback is variable (Balcazar, Hopkins & Suarez, 1986). Feedback may be effective only to the extent that appropriate rules are developed to augment the feedback. This proposition has implications for the implementation of feedback programs. Rather than allowing employees to create their own rules, desired results may be more likely if appropriate rules are provided.

TYPES OF CONTINGENCIES IN WHICH RULES OPERATE

Many of the contingencies established in OBM interventions can be described as indirect-acting (i.e., those where consequences are delayed, improbable or small and of only cumulative significance (Malott, 1989)). For example, monetary incentives based on productivity, lottery tickets for timely arrival to work, and time off for adhering to safe practices all involve contingencies which are indirect-acting.

Malott (1989) suggested that indirect-acting contingencies may be effective in the control of behavior because of rules.[2] Thus, in a feedback intervention in which the feedback is delivered once per week (i.e., a delayed consequence), the explanation for behavior change must consider feedback, *and* rules that might be stated to relate behavior to the feedback. According to Malott (1989), the statement of a rule alters the value of a delayed consequence by making its influence immediate. He suggests that stating rules sets up an immediate controlling circumstance that affects behavior until the delayed or weak consequence can exert more direct control.

In order to illustrate the possible effects of "indirect-acting" contingencies and rules, we will consider a typical OBM study. Brown and Redmon (1989) investigated the influence of group reinforcement contingencies on staff use of scheduled sick days in a child treatment facility. The intervention involved several elements: (1) staff who worked together in a single cottage formed a group; (2) if members of the group either had perfect attendance or scheduled sick leave at least 24 hours in advance, their names were entered in a lottery; (3) a lottery drawing was held every two weeks and one person from each cottage that met criterion received a prize through the drawing; and (4) in cottages where staff exhibited excellent performance (usually good attendance and compliance with scheduling policies), two names were drawn in the lottery. The results indicated that the contingency worked very well; significant reductions in the use of unscheduled sick leave time were noted in each cottage over a five-month period.

In the Brown and Redmon study, the individual, daily consequences of the target behaviors of either coming to work (instead of staying home) or calling in sick 24 hours in advance were far removed from the prizes awarded through the lottery every two weeks. Additionally, the target behaviors occurred away from group social influences in that no peers, who would lose eligibility for the lottery, were present at the time the employee made the decision to call in or come to work. Thus, it is clear that the effects of the lottery were delayed and weak.

A complete analysis of this intervention in terms of rule control would assess the extent to which subjects described the contingencies and acted accordingly. Subjects might have stated "If I call in before the deadline, my cottage will still be eligible for the drawing and people will not lose their chance to win a prize." Or, conversely, "If I don't call in by the deadline, my cottage will lose its eligibility and everybody will be upset with me." Such statements made at the time the decision had to be made might alter the function of existing stimuli which would evoke the call or the act of leaving for work. Unfortunately, these researchers, like many others in the OBM field, did not interview subjects to discover the types of rules that might have been devised and used or attempt to devise formal "rule-based" reminders (e.g., reminder cards) in the home environment to more formally manipulate rule effects. Thus, we are left to surmise that the delayed consequences somehow influenced the target behaviors without explicit evidence of the mechanism by which this influence occurred.

In the above case, the statement of a rule could have altered the value of getting approval from a supervisor for time off, or it may have altered the effects of the time of day (i.e., the deadline for calling in), or both. In any case, the target behavior could have been made more likely as a result of the rule statement.

RULE-GOVERNED BEHAVIOR: IMPLICATIONS FOR OBM RESEARCH

Use of analyses of contingencies based on rules raises several possibilities for future OBM research. At least two techniques should be considered: (1) interviews of subjects after the experiment to determine the nature of rules used, and (2) direct manipulation of rules along with other elements of an intervention to assess their effects on performance.

Human operant researchers have been encouraged to include verbal reports in their results and to supplement direct observation of overt behaviors with verbal reports (Perone, 1988). Perone suggests that more use be made of self-report data and describes four possible categories: (1) reports of observations of own behavior where subjects observe their own performance as a substitute for observation by others (e.g., self-recording); (2) verbal responses to a standard set of questions that produce a measure of a global characteristic of behavior (e.g., job satisfaction); (3) verbal reports as primary data and not as representative of other events, such as cases where subjects' verbal reports are the target of change (e.g., training accurate verbal reports of environmental events); and (4) self reports used for explanatory purposes in understanding behavior patterns (e.g., asking subjects what rules they devised to control their responding on a task). A similar view was taken by Mawhinney (1985) who suggested that operant theorists might benefit from more intensive study and analysis of attributions that may enhance or interfere with control by contingencies of reinforcement.

All of the above approaches have been used to some extent in the human operant literature and, in some cases, in OBM studies. Many OBM researchers have relied on self-recording of performance as a primary dependent variable (e.g., Caplin, Edelstein, & Redmon, 1988); however, few have measured global indicators of subject response such as job satisfaction; and few have questioned subjects as to their private verbal behavior in explaining the effects of overt contingencies. Adding one or more of the above methods could improve the clarity and extensiveness of analyses in OBM research.

Of course, the use of verbal reports opens researchers to some potential criticisms. How can we be sure that verbal reports are accurate? As Perone indicated, some reports of verbal behavior rely, perhaps too heavily, on anecdotal information or general impressions, and not measures shown to be valid and reliable. He goes on to say, that "The eventual goal would be to develop measures of verbal behavior that are as refined as our measures of nonverbal behavior," and concludes that, "At present, we may be too uncritical in accepting anecdotal verbal data" (p. 74).

POSSIBLE PITFALLS IN RULE-GOVERNED ANALYSES

While the purpose of this paper is to advocate an increase in OBM analyses involving rules, OBM researchers should learn from the mistakes of other behavior analysts and avoid overuse of this concept. Rule-governed behavior should not come to be a catch-all concept invoked when no other behavioral explanation is viable. Unfortunately the term rule has been used in a nontechnical way by the lay public and behavior analysts, and such nontechnical definitions are not easily replaced. It is recommended that researchers begin any discussion of rules by presenting the functional definition of rules (function-altering, contingency specifying stimuli), and proceed accordingly.

Researchers also are cautioned against *replacing* the analysis of underlying controlling contingencies with simple reference to the existence of rules (for a discussion of this issue, see Brownstein & Shull, 1985). Rules are *descriptions* of underlying contingencies; they do not control the behavior. The stimuli which are altered by the rules control the behavior, and those stimuli must be described in a functional analysis. To say that a rule controls behavior is to present an incomplete analysis.

Another word of caution concerns the phrase "rule-governed behavior." As Blakely and Schlinger (1987) point out, the phrase is a misnomer given the precise definition of the term rule. In their words, "behavior is not 'governed' by rules in the sense that it is evoked by them. Rather, behavior is evoked by the events described by the rules (e.g., CSSs and S^Ds). If anything is 'governed' or determined by rules, it is the functional relation between these events and behavior" (p. 186). Because the phrase "rule-governed" is embedded in behavioral vocabulary, these authors do not suggest replacing it, but do caution against misinterpreting what is being governed in rule-governed behavior. Additionally, analysts are encouraged to avoid cognitive-like references to rules that are stated covertly. Because rules often are stated privately, they are difficult to observe directly and, thus, pose a problem for an experimental analysis. However, as Skinner (1974) points out, a lack of public agreement as to the existence of a stimulus does not negate that stimulus as a potential controlling variable. Private events should not be excluded from functional analyses. Rules, whether covertly or overtly stated, may be part of the controlling variables for organizational behavior; and their inclusion in analyses may lead to more complete and accurate explanations of behavior.

CONCLUSION

This paper argues that rules play a role in the control of organizational behavior and should be included in the analyses of such behavior. However, a functional definition of rules must be adhered to if this concept is to contribute to the field of OBM. Although precise term usage may be considered an academic exercise by practitioners whose main concern is changing behavior, accurate usage has implications for application. When behavioral principles are described loosely, they are often used loosely and, thus, ineffectively. If OBM is to prosper, it must establish and maintain a good reputation, including the ability to produce meaningful behavior changes and the use of sound operant analyses to explain those changes.

Finally, if the controlling variables for a successful intervention are misunderstood (i.e., due to a superficial or inaccurate functional analysis), research will not contribute to the technology of behavior change. Practitioners benefit from more precise analyses in that this enables them to develop more effective interventions (Duncan & Bruwelheide, 1986; Peterson, 1982). Precise terminology and analyses lead to precise practices.

NOTES

1. It should be noted that Cerutti (1989) contends that insensitivity to schedule control should not be used as evidence for the existence of rule-governed behavior and suggested that factors other than self instruction may account for such effects.

2. Although Malott suggests that rules work to make indirect-acting contingencies more effective, he does not agree that this effect is achieved primarily through the function-altering means proposed by Schlinger and Blakely. Rather, he contends that statement of a rule creates aversive stimulation that is escaped when the rule is complied with. Thus, Malott relies on a two factor theory of reinforcement. For a discussion of two factor theory versus correlation based theories of reinforcement see Baum (1973). See Malott (1992) elsewhere in this issue for more details of his approach to rule governed behavior.

REFERENCES

Balcazar, F., Hopkins, B. & Suarez, Y. (1986). A critical, objective review of performance feedback. *Journal of Organizational Behavior Management, 7,* 65-75.

Baum, W. M. (1973). The Correlation Based Law of Effect. *Journal of Experimental Analysis of Behavior, 20,* 137-153.

Bentall, R. P., Lowe, C. F. & Beasty, A. (1985). The role of verbal behavior in human learning: II. Developmental differences. *Journal of the Experimental Analysis of Behavior, 43,* 165-181.

Blakely, E., & Schlinger, H. (1987). Rules: Function-altering contingency-specifying stimuli. *The Behavior Analyst, 10,* 183-187.

Brown, N., & Redmon, W. K. (1989). The effects of a group reinforcement contingency on staff use of unscheduled sick leave. *Journal of Organizational Behavior Management, 10*(2), 3-17.

Brownstein, A. J., & Shull, R. L. (1985). A rule for the use of the term "rule-governed" behavior. *The Behavior Analyst, 8,* 265-267.

Caplin, J. P., Edelstein, B., & Redmon, W. K. (1988). Performance feedback and goal setting to improve mental health center staff productivity. *Journal of Organizational Behavior Management, 9*(2), 35-58.

Cerutti, D. T. (1989). Discrimination theory of rule-governed behavior. *Journal of the Experimental Analysis of Behavior, 51,* 259-276.

Duncan, P. K., & Bruwelheide, L. R. (1986). Feedback: Use and possible behavioral functions. *Journal of Organizational Behavior Management, 7*(3/4), 91-114.

Huber, V. L. (1986). The interplay of goals and promises of pay-for-performance on individual and group performance: An operant interpretation. *Journal of Organizational Behavior Management, 7,* 45-64.

Leander, J. D., Lippman, L. G., & Meyer, M. E. (1968). Fixed interval performance as related to subjects' verbalizations of the reinforcement contingency. *Psychological Record, 18,* 469-474.

Malott, R. W. (1989). The achievement of evasive goals: Control by rules describing contingencies that are not direct acting. In S. C. Hayes (Ed.), *Rule-governed behavior: Cognition, contingencies, and instructional control* (pp. 269-324). New York: Plenum Press.

Malott, R. W. (1992). A theory of rule-governed behavior and organizational behavior management. *Journal of Organizational Behavior Management.*

Mawhinney, T. C. (1975). Operant terms and concepts in the description of individual work behavior: Some problems of interpretation, application and evaluation. *Journal of Applied Psychology, 60,* 704-712.

Mawhinney, T. C. (1985). Learning what's inside the teaching machine from the outside: Operant technology applied to cognitive phenomena. *Journal of Management, 11* (1), 134-139.

Perone, M. (1988). Laboratory lore and research practices in the experimental analysis of human behavior: Use and abuse of subjects' verbal reports. *The Behavior Analyst, 11,* 71-75.

Peterson, N. (1982). Feedback is not a new principle of behavior. *The Behavior Analyst, 5,* 101-102.

Schlinger, H., & Blakely, E. (1987). Function-altering effects of contingency-specifying stimuli. *The Behavior Analyst, 10,* 41-45.

Skinner, B. F. (1969). *Contingencies of reinforcement: A theoretical analysis.* Englewood Cliffs, NJ: Prentice-Hall.

Skinner, B. F. (1974). *About behaviorism.* New York: Alfred A. Knopf.

Vaughan, M. (1989). Rule-governed behavior in behavior analysis: A theoretical and experimental history. In S. C. Hayes (Ed.), *Rule-governed behavior: Cognition, contingencies and instructional control* (pp. 97-118). New York: Plenum Press.

COMMENTS ON MALOTT'S THEORY PAPER AND THE THEORETICAL ANALYSIS BY MALOTT, SHIMAMUNE, AND MALOTT

Much Ado About Something: Comments on Papers by Malott and Malott, Shimamune, and Malott

Donald M. Baer

I agree entirely with them (Malott, 1992; Malott, Shimamune, & Malott, 1992): That is, I note the following:

Many, many organizations seem to control the behavior of their members,

not by reinforcing and punishing appropriately, which is clumsy, costly, inefficient, and probably aversive in many cultures, but by stating enough rules to effect the task analysis of the job the organization wants done, and

by occasionally offering reinforcers to members, paired with suffi-

Donald M. Baer is affiliated with the University of Kansas.

ciently public verbal statements of how often those members had followed the rules, and

by occasionally offering reprimands and imposing dismissals on members, paired with sufficiently public verbal statements of how often these members had broken or ignored the rules.

This kind of control is at risk to the extent that:

the rules are not an adequate task analysis of the job that the organization wants those workers to do, and

to the extent that the rules can be broken without punishment, and

to the extent that the organization's members know how often or rarely the rules have been broken without punishment.

I have only two criticisms of the Malott et al. manuscripts:

First, what is gained by offering as lengthy and detailed an account of rule-governance as they do, rather than a one page summary like the above? I ask not a rhetorical question, but a functional one: I would be glad to read an answer, and I am prepared to learn from that answer (but do not guarantee that I will). However, the two manuscripts sent for review are not the answer; perhaps the answer is implicit in them, but if so, it is too implicit for me to see.

Second, I suggest that these two discussions are limited severely to only the third of any organization's three implicit rules:

Rule 1:   Survive.
Rule 2:   Grow.
Rule 3:   Do the jobs that define the mission of the organization, but never so well that growth is curtailed or survival is threatened.

In amplification of Rule 3, which has been noted by many analysts from a variety of theoretical viewpoints, consider an example:

Public schools are organizations created to educate our children sufficiently for our survival as a society in a competitive, technological world. They do not behave as if a solution to that problem were well known, although it is indeed very well known. Instead, they succeed at teaching just enough of our society's children just enough to maintain their funding as an agency likely to solve that problem, and fail to teach just enough of our society's children just enough to make a case for better funding–for expansion, specialization, more personnel, more training of those personnel, more space, more bureaucracy, and more equipment and facilities. If the schools were to use the 20-year-old, well demonstrated behavioral technology that would accomplish virtually all of their public mission, they would find that they had to shrink, not grow. That would violate Rule 2. It won't happen. Their personnel increasingly will not even know of the solution, and any inadvertent exposure to what can be seen to be part of it will prove aversive to them.

What will happen has also been noted repeatedly by various observers:

Growth will progressively hinder the organization in accomplishing even that fraction of its mission necessary to keep its society's confidence and funding, but Rule 2 will prevail even so, and the organization will eventually become so large and complex, and hence so ineffective, that it will be abandoned or largely supplanted–a functional suicide. Doesn't that look familiar?

My point is only that what the Malotts and Shimamune have explained is part of the problem, and an interesting part of the problem, but the least of the problem. Still, it deserves an explanation, and this is a good one.

I have argued this before, and more fully, as Chapter 31 in the *Handbook of Behavior Therapy in Education*, edited by Witt, Elliott, and Gresham, published by Plenum in 1988.

REFERENCES

Malott, R. W. (1992). A theory of rule governed behavior and organizational behavior management. *Journal of Organizational Behavior Management, 12*(2).

Malott, R. W., Shimamune, S., & Malott, M. E. (1992). Rule-governed behavior and organizational behavior management: An analysis of the literature. *Journal of Organizational Behavior Management, 12* (2).

For Parsimony's Sake:
Comments on Malott's
"A Theory of Rule-Governed Behavior and Organizational Behavior Management"

William M. Baum

William M. Baum is associated with the University of New Hampshire.

Malott has undertaken a worthwhile project: clarifying the importance of rules in human behavior in real environments, such as the workplace. His conclusion that much behavior in the workplace is rule-governed or at least potentially rule-governed and that more effective control over workers' behavior can be achieved by contingencies combined with rules than by contingencies alone seems well founded. The way that the author arrived at these conclusions, however, is suspect if not seriously flawed. The paper illustrates well how someone can arrive at correct conclusions by questionable arguments.

The most serious error is the author's insistence on immediacy as part of the definition of reinforcement. We are told that contingencies involving delays larger than some duration are to be called "indirect." We are told, however, that "reinforcers" delivered at such long durations cannot reinforce. This is a conceptual muddle. Presumably if the delayed reinforcer cannot reinforce, then the "reinforcer" could be omitted from the contingency with no effect. This, however, would mean that the contingency was not a contingency after all. The author himself admits the obvious: If the promised delayed reinforcer were omitted, the employees would soon cease to respond to the rules.

The contingency exists no matter how great the delay between behavior it requires and receipt of the consequence(s) it controls. Sex produces

William M. Baum

William M. Baum is associated with the University of New Hampshire.

a baby at a delay of nine months. There is nothing unreal about that contingency. People keep promises after months or years; there is nothing unreal about those contingencies either.

It is true, however, that delayed consequences tend to be ineffective. That is the basis of problems in self-control–choices between relatively immediate small consequences *versus* delayed large consequences. When we choose the immediate consequence to our long-term detriment, we are said to act impulsively. When we choose the delayed consequence to our long-term benefit, we are said to exhibit self-control.

Malott does not appear to appreciate self-control theory. He himself points out that when large consequences seem ineffective, their inability to affect behavior can always be traced to delay. In his examples, however, he focusses on only one alternative in the choice. The reason that people overeat and gain weight is that eating produces immediate reinforcement whereas the weight gain is delayed. The idea of small incremental changes is unnecessary; delay covers it, provided you remember that every problem in self-control involves choices occurring through time and delayed, but correlated, consequences that also occur through time.

The author goes on to suggest that when rules are introduced, delay becomes irrelevant. This argument does not fit existing facts. Whatever role rules play in conjunction with delay, humans respond to choices involving immediate and delayed consequences as though they follow a rule which compares the value of an immediate amount of something and the value of a delayed amount discounted by some proportion. Whether an alternative response with a delayed consequence is preferred depends on whether its value (depending on both amount and delay) is greater than the value of immediate consequences from other choices (Rachlin, 1989).

Rules are a means by which delayed consequences can be made more effective. Therein lies their great value and their indispensability for culture. I need not become addicted to cocaine to avoid taking it. I need not see genetic defects in my descendants to avoid marrying my sister. The consequences are delayed, but the rules of my culture insure that I will behave adaptively with respect to them.

A rule is a verbal discriminative stimulus. That is all. Its presence makes it likely that I will behave adaptively with respect to delayed consequences.

As a discriminative stimulus, however, the rule is related to more consequences than just the delayed consequence. Other contingencies are involved, because we are taught to follow rules from early childhood. It is an essential part of growing up in a culture, of what people call "socialization." It is also called obedience, cooperation, good citizenship, and so on. As a general learned skill, rule-following is reinforced by parents and significant others with approval and tokens, reinforcers that can be delivered immediately. Failing to follow rules is also frequently punished. Parents, for example, begin with commands (Go wash your hands), proceed to requests (Please help with the groceries), and then to advice (You should marry Mabel)–all rules, all pointing to contingencies having to do with consequences from the parent. The sequence shifts the child from stricter to looser contingencies. Advice represents an important step, because advice concerns delayed consequences to the child (of marrying Mabel). Even advice, however, is usually given with the expectation that it will be followed and that following it will be reinforced not only at a delay but more immediately by the approval of the advice-giver.

There would be no rule-following if there were not also rule-making–another type of operant behavior shaped up by growing up in a culture. What is the reinforcement for rule-making? We often say it is for the directed person's "own good," with some justice, because of the reinforcement, immediate and delayed, for rule-following, but there's always something in it for the rule-maker, too. Rule-making is reinforced also with approval and tokens, when we are encouraged to help others. We pay consultants large sums of money to tell us what to do (i.e., make rules). In the workplace, the reinforcers for rule-making are obvious, productivity and profit.

The important point is that rule-making is the giving of verbal discriminative stimuli, rule-following is the control of operant behavior by the verbal discriminative stimuli. In addition to the delayed reinforcers that the rules are all about, there are or have been more immediate social reinforcers. Malott seems to have been led to postulate additional factors (e.g., aversive preconditions established by rules) by a failure to appreciate rule-following in the context of the individual's overall history of reinforcement.

The view I have described requires no new concepts to explain why successful management in the workplace depends on correct use of rules. No need to talk about direct and indirect contingencies; immediate and delayed consequences will do. No need to talk about "analogues." No need to overlook the importance of conditional and token reinforcers. No need to talk about "rule control" as if it were something different from stimulus control. No need to talk about "establishing operations."

Malott's theory advocates a complication of more parsimonious descriptions already well developed in the literature. Unless the new theory accounts for some data better, there is no reason to adopt it. Whether the theory should guide future research in the area should depend on how it performs relative to accepted theory. If they make different predictions, then they can be tested empirically; if they make the same predictions, then parsimony is to be preferred.

REFERENCE

Rachlin, H. (1989). *Judgement, decision, and choice*. New York: W. H. Freeman.

An Important First Step, but Not the Last Word on Rule-Governed Behavior and OBM: Comments on Papers by Malott and Malott, Shimamune, and Malott

Howard Rachlin

My comments concern three aspects of the two papers by Malott (1992) and colleagues (Malott, Shimamune, & Malott, 1992) regarding theoretical and empirical aspects of rule-governed behavior and OBM: (1) practical and empirical, (2) conceptual, and (3) its connection with the concept of self-control.

PRACTICAL/EMPIRICAL

The overall empirical points made in the two papers are well taken. Rule governance is an important consideration in almost all areas of human behavior. I also agree with the implication of Figure 1 in the theory paper that the stronger the underlying contingencies, the easier it is to follow the rule that describes them.

Malott's solution to the problem of failure of behavioral control, as I gather it from both papers, is to alter the contingencies from the ineffective to the effective category and then support the changed contingencies with easy-to-follow rules. I agree with this suggestion as well.

My disagreement comes down to this: in the most complex and intractable cases of poor organizational- and self-management it will not

---

Howard Rachlin is affiliated with State University of New York at Stony Brook.

85

be possible, and even where possible it might not be a good idea, to change the contingencies. It may well be too costly to have supervisors provide the frequent feedback that is recommended; even where not costly it might generate a "big-brother-is-watching-you" attitude. This plays into the hands of critics like Schwartz, Schuldenfrei and Lacey (1978) who see operant psychology as factory psychology. The trick would be with the baseline contingencies *as they are* in nature or in an organization, to provide better rules. The key to making better rules, I believe, will lie in techniques that make good contact with the prevalent contingencies and perhaps with *temporary* feedback changes, faded out once the more global (hence "ineffective") contingencies come to control behavior. Dieting is a case in point. The natural contingencies for dieting are notoriously ineffective and rules, hard to follow. But permanent contingency changes are also hard to maintain hence the general ineffectiveness of dieting. The difficulty lies, I believe, not in the initial change of contingencies. That's the easy part. As I think is now generally recognized, even in the popular culture, the difficulty lies in preventing slippage when the contingencies revert to the natural ("ineffective") ones. Slippage may be prevented via a good set of imposed rules upon the natural contingencies which after all must prevail. In OBM this most likely concerns the status of effective interventions by OBM researchers or practitioners during their intervention as compared to after their departure.

CONCEPTUAL

On the more conceptual end, the papers oversimplify things by taking continua and making dichotomies out of them: probability and delay, are both obviously continua (a repeated probability being only a variable rather than fixed delay). But rule-governed and contingency-governed behavior also lie on a temporal continuum. All behavior is in a sense rule-governed and all, in a sense, contingency-governed. Even a rat's single reinforced lever press may be seen as an instance of a very complex set of rules governing muscular movement. Ultimately, even building a house may be viewed as a very long-duration operant. In the course of a contractor building a development the building of a single house may well indeed be a behavioral unit, reinforced as immediately (relative to the time the individual response takes) as a lever press. Otherwise, insisting on a more detailed analysis, we would have to worry about the connection between the money the contractor gets and eventual primary reinforcement (eating a spaghetti dinner, say). Spending money, too, reflects an implicit but very complex set of rules. (Try giving cash to a pigeon.)

I believe that Malott fails to give serious consideration to the correlation-based law of effect (Baum, 1973) except indirectly as it is the basis of theoretical analyses by Mawhinney and Ford (1977) and Mawhinney and Gowen (1990). I agree with Wittgenstein (1958) that it is not possible (not even conceivable) to obey a rule just *once*. According to Malott, verbal humans differ from pigeons with respect to self-control in that they can state a rule and immediately follow it. This implies that self-control by rule following can arise upon a single occasion. Malott cites a study by Logue, Pena-Correal, Rodriguez, and Kabela (1986). In this study human subjects did not exhibit choice patterns characteristic of pigeons that exhibit matching in response to reinforcement delay; rather, the human subjects maximized. In the Logue et al. (1986) study it is possible that the correlation based law of effect controlled choice of the rule per se. Stronger evidence that rule selection arises from an informed trial and error process in which the consequences of alternative choice rules govern the eventual dominance of one rule, e.g., maximization, over another rule, e.g., matching as a default rule, is clearly evident in a study by Mawhinney (1982). Obedience to a rule is not an event (a single operant) but a *habit*, a *pattern* of events. Emergence of one pattern rather than another can arise from the operation of the correlation based law of effect.

An Individual vs. Group Contingency and Rule Analysis–Let me indicate what would be to me a better direction for an analysis of rule-governed behaviors as they relate to behavior in organizations. Consider the following version of a prisoner's dilemma game: The players are employee-X versus all the other employees. Consider the case of employee theft from the company. For the sake of argument say an individual act of stealing is worth 1 point while working in a company where employee theft is minimal is worth 10 points–due to the increased profitability, job stability and worker-supervisor relations. If the other employees don't generally steal it still pays employee-X to steal since his theft alone will hardly be noticed; he gets 11 points rather than 10. If the other employees generally do steal it *still* pays employee-X to steal because he at least gets one point rather than none.

If all the employees see things this way they each get one point instead of the ten points they each would have gotten if none of them stole. This is the standard prisoner's dilemma. How then do you get them to cooperate? The answer, I believe, lies in rule-governance aimed at developing mutual cooperation and group activity in other tasks as well as this one. A manager's graph-drawing to present evidence of the group's rate of thefts is, I think, a move in this direction (Carter, Holmstrom, Simpanen, & Melin, 1988). It relates a graphic image to a group activity. It presents the alternatives as group alternatives. It makes individuals see their own action as a group action, as a choice between 10 points (all don't steal) and 1 point (all steal) rather than between 10 and 11 or 0 and 1. The concept of group rules and group consequences is applicable to many practical human affairs in complex organizational settings.

INDIVIDUAL SELF-CONTROL

On the individual self-control level a similar problem arises. Say eating ice-cream on an individual occasion is worth 1 point while being generally thin and healthy is worth 10 points. Now the game is played between the individual at time-X and the very same individual at all other times (or at times in general–over a span of years). The same contingencies arise for cooperation and defection–with oneself and at other times. And the same role is there for rules–to shift the choice from one between the present moment's benefit versus other moments to one between being thin versus being fat. The latter choice operates wholly on an abstract level; it is in *bringing* alternatives onto that level that verbal rules have their role. (Of course, with ice-cream as opposed to stealing, it is possible, maybe even necessary, to occasionally defect, picking up 11 points in the context of general cooperation. Hence a more complex set of rules bringing ice-cream eating under control of relatively infrequent S^Ds, like birthdays, are necessary.)

REFERENCES

Baum, W. M. (1973). The Correlation Based Law of Effect. *Journal of Experimental Analysis of Behavior, 20*, 137-153.

Carter, N., Holmstrom, A., Simpanen, M., & Melin, L. (1988). Theft reduction in a grocery store product identification and graphing of losses for employees. *Journal of Applied Behavior Analysis, 21*, 385-389.

Logue, A. W., Peña-Correal, T. E., Rodriguez, M. L., & Kabela, E. (1986). Self-control in adult humans: Variation in positive reinforcer amount and delay. *Journal of the Experimental Analysis of Behavior, 46*, 159-173.

Mawhinney, T. C. (1982). Maximizing versus matching in people versus pigeons. *Psychological Reports, 50*, 267-281.

Mawhinney, T. C. & Ford, J. D. (1977). The Path-Goal Theory of Leader Effectiveness: An Operant Interpretation. *Academy of Management Review Journal, 2*, 398-411.

Mawhinney, T. C., & Gowen, C. R., III. (1990). Gainsharing and the law of effect as the matching law: A theoretical framework. *Journal of Organizational Behavior Management, 11*, 61-75.

Malott, R. W. (1992). A theory of rule governed behavior and organizational behavior management. *Journal of Organizational Behavior Management, 12* (2).

Malott, R. W., Shimamune, S., & Malott, M. E. (1992). Rule-governed behavior and organizational behavior management: An analysis of the literature. *Journal of Organizational Behavior Management, 12* (2).

Rachlin, H. (1989). *Judgement, decision, and choice*. New York: W. H. Freeman.

Schwartz, B., Schuldenfrei, R., & Lacey, H. M. (1978). Operant psychology as factory psychology. *Behaviorism, 6* (2), 229-254.

Wittgenstein, L. (1958). *Philosophical investigations*: 3rd Edition. New York: Macmillan.

Comments on Rule-Governed Behavior

Richard W. Malott
Maria E. Malott
Satoru Shimamune

COMMENTS ON BAUM'S REVIEW

This section is based on Baum (1992).

Can Delayed Outcomes Reinforce and Punish Behavior?

Baum is right: "The contingency exists no matter how great the delay between behavior it requires and receipt of the consequence(s) it controls." But if the delay in the delivery of the reinforcer is too great, it will not be a direct-acting contingency of reinforcement. The reinforcer will not reinforce the causal response, though it would reinforce other responses that just happened to precede its delivery. We suspect even the most ardent of molar theorists would not attempt to reinforce the rat's lever presses by delivering a drop of water nine months after each response. True, the water is a reinforcer. True, it is contingent on the press. But the delay is too great for it to be a reinforcement contingency.

In the same way, "Sex produces a baby at a delay of nine months. There is nothing unreal about that contingency." But being a real contingency and being a reinforcement or punishment contingency are not the same thing. We contend that the sex/baby contingency is ineffective in controlling behavior unless the person can state a rule describing that contingency. Then *if* the contingency controls behavior, it is an indirect-acting analog to a reinforcement or punishment contingency.

Richard W. Malott is affiliated with Western Michigan University. Maria E. Malott is affiliated with Performance Management Systems. Satoru Shimamune is affiliated with Sun System Inc. and Western Michigan University.

Please address requests for reprints to Richard W. Malott, Department of Psychology, Western Michigan University, Kalamazoo, MI 49008-5052.

Are Delayed Outcomes the Cause of Self-Control Problems?

We disagree with the common behavior-analytic and lay theory of self-control: "The reason that people overeat and gain weight is that eating produces immediate reinforcement whereas it produces delayed weight." Suppose every time a person overate *a single bite*, exactly one year later the person would be 10 pounds heavier. Suppose the person knew and believed the rule describing that contingency. We suggest such a person would have no weight management problems because the rule is easy to follow. Rules that produce sizable, probable outcomes are easy to follow despite the delay of that outcome. This thought experiment suggests the following: We have trouble dieting because the outcome of each individual bite is too small to punish the response. The outcome is too small although the accumulation of small outcomes over a year is large enough to punish overeating if that accumulated 10-pound weight gain were immediately contingent on the response of overeating.

Consider a real example of control by delayed outcomes; this also suggests the delay is not the cause of self-control problems: Every year, hundreds of behavior analysts submit proposals to the Association for Behavior Analysis for presentation at the annual meeting. They do so in spite of the several-months delay between that response and the reinforcer of making the presentation and in spite of the several weeks delay between that response and receipt of the reinforcer of acceptance of the paper for presentation. The delay causes little problem for self-management here, if the behavior analysts know and believe the relevant rule.

But when do these rule-governed behavior analysts submit their proposals? Just before the deadline, although this procrastination costs additional expenses and hassles in the form of overnight express mail. Why do they have this self-control problem of procrastination? Not because of the delay, but rather because the outcome of submitting the paper on any given day is too small to reinforce that response sequence. By the way, we argue that the reinforcer here is reduction of the aversive stimuli ("fear," "anxiety," or whatever) associated with the possibility of missing the deadline. For most of us, it is only when the deadline is a few days or hours away that this aversiveness becomes excessive. Then the aversiveness is great enough that reducing it reinforces proposal submission.

Concerning the "existing facts," we have suggested the following: The current human and animal experimental research on the effects of concurrently competing delays is irrelevant to most problems of self-control (Malott & Malott, 1991). This research is irrelevant because it usually involves only brief delays between the response and the reinforcer (either the terminal outcome of food or the change in an associated stimulus such as key color). This research usually involves competition between two direct-acting contingencies of reinforcement. But the delays in most real problems of self-control are way outside the laboratory range. The impact of overeating on weight gain is not felt for hours, weeks, or even years. However, the experimental literature does suggest that there must be some immediate contingency of reinforcement or punishment involved in any form of behavioral control, including self-control.

At the same time we realize that people such as financial investors do consider present value; they do "discount" their investments by some "predictable proportion"; and that proportion depends on the amount of the investment and the amount and delay of the return. However, we also suggest that the verbal, rule-governed processes underlying such "discounting" are only indirectly related to the direct-acting contingencies of reinforcement and punishment operating in the experimental laboratory and any "discounting" found there.

Does Discriminative Control Explain Rule Control?

We agree that, "Rules are a means by which delayed consequences can be made more effective." The question is how? We think it does not suffice to say, "A rule is a verbal discriminative stimulus. That is all. Its presence makes it likely that I will behave adaptively with respect to delayed consequences." We can turn the light on whenever a rat's lever press will produce a reinforcer and turn it off at other times. That light will function as a discriminative stimulus and control the lever presses, if the reinforcer is immediately contingent on the response; it will not function as a discriminative stimulus, if the reinforcer occurs nine months later. Yet if we tell you that pressing the lever once will deliver $1,000 nine months later, that statement will control your lever pressing.

Why Are Some Rules So Hard to Follow?

Of course rule-governance is a culturally acquired repertoire. But the question is why are some rules so hard to follow, whereas others are not. Few will have problems with the rule describing the $1,000 lever press because it describes an outcome that is sizable and probable, though delayed. Many have trouble with rules describing contingencies with small but cumulatively significant outcomes such as those prohibiting the use of cocaine, nicotine, alcohol, fat, sugar, salt, and cholesterol. For example, "Don't eat fudge sundaes because they contain fat, sugar, and cholesterol that will harm your health, at least if you eat them too often." And many people have trouble with rules describing contingencies with improbable outcomes such as those recommending safe working, safe driving, and safe sex. People have trouble although those improbable outcomes may be immediate.

How Do We Manage Our Performance
When No One Is Looking?

We generally agree (Malott, 1989) that "We are taught to follow rules from early childhood. It is an essential part of growing up in a culture." Parents use direct-acting contingencies of reinforcement and punishment to support their children's compliance with rules; it is straightforward why the children should comply with the rules, when the parents are around to maintain those direct-acting performance-management contingencies. But this seems less straightforward to us: Why would those direct-acting parental contingencies produce control by rules describing delayed outcomes *when no one is there* to enforce those contingencies? The parental contingencies of childhood also seem to provide less than a straightforward answer to the following: Why do people have trouble following rules describing improbable and small although cumulatively significant outcomes? It is to deal with these more complex phenomena that we *infer* direct-acting contingencies of reinforcement and punishment; we need more than the natural external contingencies or the contingencies the parental performance managers enforce.

Why Do Many Natural Contingencies Fail
to Control Our Behavior?

Our theory suggests that an examination of ineffective natural contingencies shows those contingencies to involve improbable or small although cumulatively significant outcomes. And an examination of effective performance-management contingencies shows those contingencies to involve probable and sizable although possibly delayed outcomes if the person is verbal.

COMMENTS ON RACHLIN'S REVIEW

This section is based on Rachlin (1992).

Must We Invoke Rule-Control to Account for Organizational Behavior Management?

Both probability and delay are each continuous variables. But most performance-management concerns arise from the probability or delay of a contingent outcome being so far out on the continuum that the continuum is essentially dichotomous. For example, either the outcome is delayed so much that it cannot appreciably reinforce or punish the causal response, or it is not delayed that much. Most performance management problems do not involve delays of intermediate value, for example 15 seconds, although laboratory research on the effects of delays uses parameters only in this range. At the extreme delays involved in organizational behavior management (e.g., several months), there seems no possible reinforcement or punishment of the causal response. Therefore another mechanism must be involved to account for control exerted by such delayed outcomes. We propose rule control as the mechanism. However, *even rule control must ultimately be based on direct-acting contingencies of reinforcement and punishment* (but those direct-acting contingencies are not the obvious natural ones). In short, we find it useful to dichotomize the continua of probability and delay of outcomes. We dichotomize them into the range where those outcomes can effectively reinforce and punish the causal response and into the range where they cannot.

Are Rule Control and Contingency Control Really the Same?

It is not clear to us that "All behavior is in a sense rule-governed .... Even a rat's single reinforced lever press may be an instance of a very complex set of rules governing muscular movement." We use the generally accepted notion that rules are verbal descriptions of contingencies. So we agree that one could generate a set of rules describing the lever press contingencies and the muscle movement contingencies. But surely that should not suggest that those verbal descriptions of the contingencies are controlling the lever pressing of the nonverbal rat. The reinforcement contingencies themselves are directly controlling the behavior of the rat, without the aid of descriptive verbal rules.

Also, it is not clear to us that "All behavior is in a sense . . . contingency-governed." At least not in the sense of "Even building a house may be viewed as a very long-duration operant." The issue is, what can we consider an *operant* (the basic unit of behavior)? Can we consider such molar sequences as building a house a response class? We think not. It seems useful to restrict the meaning of *operant* to a sequence of behaviors controlled by the same reinforcing or punishing outcome.

For example, consider the rat's lever press as an operant. The lever press consists of a chain of responses: looking up from the water dipper, walking toward the lever, raising above the lever, and lowering the body and depressing the lever. This entire stimulus-response chain is controlled by the drop of water or by learned reinforcers based on that drop. This is a single operant.

But suppose we tried to establish with the rat an operant consisting of a stimulus response chain that extended over several weeks. And suppose we interrupted the "chain" by sleep during the nights and by a variety of random events and activities during the days. We might carefully attempt to extend this chain across the weeks using backward chaining. And we might use a pint of water as the reinforcer at the end. But still we have no reason to expect success. The duration of the chain and the interruptions are too great; the single, though large, reinforcer at the end would not be able to reinforce the earlier links; even the mediation of learned reinforcers it might have spawned would not help enough. The chain of stimuli and responses extends over days and includes interruptions by random activities; so it will not function as an operant.

Yet the behavior of the house builder is controlled by the outcome of the completed house and the resultant pay, or at least by rules describing the relation between building the house, its completion, and the pay. If building the house is not a single operant, what is it? A *rule-governed analog to an operant*. In other words, we could train a chimpanzee to do many components of building a house, but we could not train the entire chain, using a thousand pounds of raisins as the reinforcer for the completion of the house. The contractor builds the house only with the aid of language and rule-governed behavior describing the relation between the building and the ultimate outcome. This is a *rule-governed analog to an operant* maintained by a *rule-governed analog to reinforcement*. If it were an operant maintained by reinforcement, we could train chimps to be building contractors.

Incidentally, the builder's building behavior meets many learned and unlearned reinforcers along the way; but that is not crucial to whether the entire chain holds together as an operant. That is determined by the kind of control exerted by the ultimate outcome—the completed house and the pay. If the ultimate outcome and its associated learned reinforcers maintains the chain through a direct-acting reinforcement contingency, then the chain is an operant. If the ultimate outcome maintains the sequence through a description of the house building/reinforcement contingency, then the sequence is a rule-governed analogue to an operant.

Can the Correlation-Based Law of Effect Account for Control by Extremely Delayed Outcomes?

Rachlin is concerned about whether "it is . . . possible . . . to obey a single rule just *once*." This may be a different issue from how specific rules come to control behavior. And how specific rules come to control behavior is a different issue from how rules in general can come to control behavior. Most of us have a history that will allow the following rule to control our behavior on the single occasion we hear it: "Don't touch that hot stove, it'll burn you." On other occasions, we may come to infer a rule because of repeated successful and unsuccessful (trial and error) interactions with our environment; however, probably more often "authorities" simply tell us the rules.

Still a separate issue is how do we account for the control of rules describing outcomes delayed by several weeks. Can we extrapolate from the animal research on the correlation based law of effect where the delays are a matter of minutes? In other words, can we treat contingencies involving delays of several weeks as if they were direct-acting contingencies of reinforcement? Everything we know about the rapid decrements in the effectiveness of delayed reinforcement suggests not. The burden rests with the advocates of such analyses. They must show with lower animals that the correlation based law of effect applies under these parameters: The reinforcers and behaviors are distributed over intervals of weeks; no single reinforcers occur more frequently than once a week; and the animal is removed from the test chamber every night.

Are There No Easy Solutions to Performance Problems?

We agree with Rachlin: There may be cases where performance management is not cost effective. And there may be cases where performance management generates problems of public relations. And we agree that it would be wonderful, if we could convert rules that are hard to follow to rules that are easy to follow, "perhaps with *temporary* feedback changes, faded out once the more global (hence "ineffective") contingencies come to control behavior." Unfortunately, we have not been able to find any evidence that anyone has a technology that reliably produces this wonderful state of affairs. Nor have we found evidence that "Slippage may be prevented via a good set of imposed rules upon the natural contingencies"; of course, it would be wonderful magic if we could get all us back-sliding dieters to learn and follow such "a good set of imposed" rules.

Yes it would be wonderful if we could get people to work for the well-being of the group by getting them to follow rules supporting altruistic behavior, although the organizational contingencies support selfish behavior. Because we know of no empirical or theoretical evidence that this wonderful condition is achievable, we will continue to recommend changing the contingencies (including indirect-acting contingencies) so they simultaneously support work for the well-being of the group as well as work for the well-being of the individual worker.

Similarly it would be wonderful if we could get people to eat in a healthy manner, simply by stating rules describing the small but cumulatively deleterious effects of eating ice cream. Or by repeating those rules one hundred times. It would be wonderful if some such procedure would shift people to the choice between one bite of ice cream and a life time of being fat rather than between one bite of ice cream and an indiscernible increment in weight. The first choice would control healthy behavior readily, the second does not. But because we know of no empirical or theoretical evidence that this wonderful condition is achievable, we will continue to recommend changing the contingencies (including indirect-acting contingencies) so they support healthy behavior.

COMMENTS ON BAER'S REVIEW

This section is based on Baer (1992).

Why Do Organizations Often Fail to Manage the Performance of Their Employees?

We can summarize much of the *Journal of Organizational Behavior Management*, the *Journal of Applied Behavior Analysis*, and the *Journal of the Experimental Analysis of Behavior*, when we say behavior is controlled by its consequences. But that should not suggest we gain nothing by offering the journals as explication of the law of effect.

Similarly, Baer can summarize much of our writing on rule-governed behavior in organizations in a one-page abstract. But that should not suggest we gain nothing by offering a more detailed account. In fact, it looks like we need this additional article to clarify the complex issues our previous articles obviously failed to make clear to the commentors.

Here is the crucial point our two papers seemed not to have effectively highlighted: The organizational behavior-management contingencies that control compliance with organizational rules are usually not the direct-acting contingencies of punishment to which Baer refers when listing the factors that put rule-control at risk. They are often indirect-acting analogs to punishment and avoidance. Furthermore, the major reason rule-control is at risk is that organizational behavior-management contingencies often involve outcomes for each individual instance of an act that are too small to reinforce or punish that act although the accumulation of those outcomes is clearly a reinforcer or aversive condition. For example, "Work hard all the time and you will accelerate up the organizational chart." But no individual instance of working hard appreciably affects that acceleration. So control by that rule is at risk.

How Can We Help Organizations Achieve Their Missions?

We agree with Baer that perfect behavior management of the workers of an organization does not guarantee the organization will accomplish its defined mission. To guarantee such a result, the outcomes of the workers' behavior must contribute to the accomplishment of a set of objectives that lead to the ultimate goal of accomplishing that mission. We have addressed this problem elsewhere (Malott & Garcia, 1987; Shimamune & Malott, 1991, May). Whether performance management is the "least of the problem[s]" of organizations, it is not a trivial problem. And, although we believe, behavior analysis in general and organizational behavior analysis in particular is amiss in neglecting goal-directed systems design, we do not expect every article in the field to address this problem.

Why Do Organizations Resist Adopting Behavioral Technology?

No doubt individual workers have resisted more efficient and effective technology for fear that the new technology would make their job obsolete or at least cause their job to be degraded. Teachers' initial resistance to programmed instruction is an example. But we suspect that few organizations have the hidden agenda of sand bagging the adoption of such technology for fear that the technology would limit growth. For example, how many parents resist behavioral technology applied to the management of the behavior of their family members because it will limit the growth of their family (their organization)? Instead, our observation is this: The management of organizations resist adopting behavioral technology because applied behavior analysts do not make effective use of what we know about how to diffuse technology (Backer, Liberman, & Kuehnel, 1986; Bailey, 1991; Lindsley, 1991; Pumroy & McIntire, 1991; Redmon, 1991; Stoltz, 1981).

Why Do Adopting Organizations Fail to Maintain Behavioral Technology?

Even when management or individuals enthusiastically accept behavioral technology, they rarely implement it; and when they implement it, they rarely maintain it. Why? Because of the factors we've considered in our other two papers in this issue (Malott, 1992; Malott, Shimamune, & Malott, 1992)–the rules describing the use of performance management technology are hard to follow; they specify outcomes that are small and of only cumulative significance; most individual instances of reinforcement or extinction used by the performance manager have no appreciable impact on behavior of the client; the changes in the client's behavior are too small and only cumulative and thus do not reinforce the use of behavioral technology by the performance manager.

Behavior analysts, as well as lay people, blame the victims for failing to do what they clearly need to do to achieve a goal. They say the victims do not really want to achieve the goal, or else they would do what needs to be done to achieve it. For example, even behavior-analytic professors say the reason high-risk college students do not study hard enough is because they do not value the grades or knowledge that will result from studying. Such simplistic forms of victim blaming result from a failure to appreciate the difficulty of following rules that describe contingencies involving small but cumulatively significant outcomes (e.g., students procrastinate because putting off studying for just a few more minutes will not matter, not necessarily because they don't value good grades or knowledge).

Just as we should avoid blaming victims at an individual level for failing to do what needs to be done, we also should avoid blaming victims and the organizational-management level for failing to adopt our technology. Their failure often stems from the difficulty of following rules that are hard to follow and from other sources, rather than a fear of success.

REFERENCES

Backer, T. E., Liberman, R. P., & Kuehnel, T. G. (1986). Dissemination and adoption of innovative psychosocial interventions. Journal of Consulting and Clinical Psychology, *54*, 111-118.

Baer, D. M. (1992). Much ado about something: Comments on papers by Malott and Malott, Shimamune, and Malott. *Journal of Organizational Behavior Management, 12* (2).

Bailey, J. S. (1991). Making behavior analysis requires different talk. *Journal of Applied Behavior Analysis, 24*, 445-448.

Baum, W. M. (1992). For parsimony's sake: Comments on Malott's "A theory of rule-governed behavior and organizational behavior management." *Journal of Organizational Behavior Management, 12* (2).

Lindsley, O. R. (1991). From technical jargon to plain English for application. *Journal of Applied Behavior Analysis, 24*, 449-454.

Malott, R. W. (1989). The achievement of evasive goals: Control by rules describing indirect-acting contingencies. In S. C. Hayes (Ed.), *Rule-governed behavior: Cognition, contingencies, and instructional control.* (pp. 269-322). New York: Plenum.

Malott, R. W. (1992). A theory of rule-governed behavior and organizational behavior management. *Journal of Organizational Behavior Management*, this issue.

Malott, R. W. & Garcia, M. E. (1987). A goal directed model approach for the design of human performance systems. *Journal of Organizational Behavior Management, 9*, 125-159.

Malott, R. W., & Malott, M. E. (1991). Private events and rule-governed behavior. In L. J. Hayes & P. N. Chase (Eds.) *Dialogues on verbal behavior.* (pp. 237-254). Reno, NV: Context Press.

Malott, R. W., Shimamune, S., & Malott, M. E. (1992). Rule-governed behavior and organizational behavior management: An analysis of the literature. *Journal of Organizational Behavior Management, 12* (2).

Pumroy, D. K. & McIntire, R. (1991). Behavior analysis/modification for everyone. *Journal of Behavioral Education, 1*, 283-293.

Rachlin, H. (1992). An important first step, but not the last word on rule-governed behavior and OBM: Comments on papers by Malott and Malott, Shimamune, and Malott. *Journal of Organizational Behavior Management, 12* (2).

Redmon, W. K. (1991) Pinpointing the technological fault in applied behavior analysis. *Journal of Applied Behavior Analysis, 24*, 441-444.

Shimamune, S. & Malott, R. W. (1991, May). *A goal-directed systems design for the Association for Behavior Analysis.* Poster presented at the meeting of the Association for Behavior Analysis: International, Atlanta, GA.

Stoltz, S. B. (1981). Adoption of innovations from applied behavior analysis: "Does anybody care?" *Journal of Applied Behavior Analysis, 14*, 491-505.

A THEORETICAL ANALYSIS
OF RULE-GOVERNED BEHAVIOR
AND AN OBM INTERVENTION
WITHIN STRUCTURAL
AND CULTURAL CONSTRAINTS

Rule-Governed Behavior
and Organizational
Behavior Management:
An Analysis of Interventions

Richard W. Malott
Satoru Shimamune
Maria Emma Malott

SUMMARY. A theoretical analysis of research in organizational behavior management shows: (a) The natural contingencies usually involved outcomes that were too small or too improbable to control the target behavior; (b) None of the interventions involved adding

Richard W. Malott is affiliated with Western Michigan University. Satoru Shimamune is affiliated with Sun System Inc. and Western Michigan University. Maria Emma Malott is affiliated with Performance Management Systems.

contingencies of reinforcement and punishment like those studied in the animal laboratory. Instead the interventions involved adding contingencies analogous to the contingencies of the laboratory. These intervention contingencies were analogs, because their outcomes were too delayed to reinforce or punish the target behavior. But they did support the target performance. (c) We inferred direct-acting escape and punishment contingencies to account for the effectiveness of the intervention contingencies. (d) Probably the intervention contingencies would not have controlled the target behavior had the participants not been able to state rules describing those contingencies.

Malott (1991) has argued that we should not make literal extrapolations from the direct-acting contingencies of the animal laboratory to the indirect-acting contingencies of the organizational culture or the organizational behavior manager. This is because the contingencies of the organization often involve outcomes that are too delayed to reinforce or punish the target behavior. Instead we should look at the target behavior as governed by rules the participant uses to describe those indirect-acting, delayed contingencies. (See glossary for terminology relevant to this article.)

GENERAL TRENDS

To find out what type of intervention contingencies are used in the field of organizational behavior management, we reviewed the articles published in the *Journal of Organization Behavior Management* and the *Journal of Applied Behavior Analysis* during the decade of 1980 to 1989. We selected all articles that showed effective behavior modification interventions with normal adults working in organizations, excluding articles that focused on behavior change of clients and on evaluation of training programs.

For each article, we selected the part of the intervention that seemed most crucial and analyzed the relevant behavioral contingencies. Of the 48 studies we analyzed, 98% involved the explicit manipulation of contingencies; only one study (2%) did not (Kello, Geller, Rice, & Bryant, 1988).

Of the 47 studies that involved explicit manipulation of contingencies, 100% used indirect-acting contingencies. These contingencies specified outcomes that were sizeable and probable but delayed. In other words, none of the intervention contingencies were direct-acting contingencies that would reinforce or punish the causal response.

The majority of the intervention contingencies involved analogs to reinforcement and analogs to avoidance. For representative examples, see: Gaetani, Hoxeng, and Austin (1985) who used a pay-for-performance system to increase productivity in an automobile machining shop (this study is described in detail in the next section); Crowell, Anderson, Abel, and Sergio (1988) who used feedback and praise to modify bank tellers greeting behavior with customers; Frost, Hopkins, and Conard (1981) who used graphs and praise for good performance to increase the productivity of employees packaging products in a manufacturing department; Brown, Willis, and Reid (1981) who implemented a feedback procedure combined with supervisor approval to increase on-task behavior (social interaction and direct-care stimulation) with staff in a residential facility for multiply-handicapped, retarded persons; and Newby and Robinson (1983) who used coupons (exchangeable for free soft drinks and free candy bars) to increase on-time attendance to work.

Concerning the type of intervention used, most of the studies implemented feedback and incentives like lotteries, praise, tokens, and movie tickets. Money was not often used as an incentive. Both Balcazar, Shupert, Daniels, Mawhinney, and Hopkins (1989) and Merwin, Thomason, and Sanford (1989) also reported that the use of money incentives was rare.

We, as well as Balcazar et al. (1989) found a large number of the studies used measures of accomplishments as dependent variables, rather than behaviors. When the dependent variables are accomplishments or products of behavior rather than behavior, we can only infer the behavioral contingencies responsible for the accomplishments or products. But, if research in organizational behavior management is to contribute to the science and theory of behavior analysis by producing an understanding of the relevant contingencies, we must know what behavior and contingencies are involved. True, often behavioral technology can advance by measuring accomplishments without measuring behavior; but even then, it may be expedient to measure the behavior directly, to insure, for example, that workers do not inflate their apparent accomplishments by recycling old items from the warehouse rather than by producing new ones.

In summary of the overall review, we found that intervention contingencies used in organizational behavior management are indirect-acting behavioral contingencies that specify sizeable, probable, but delayed outcomes. Furthermore, most of these intervention contingencies consist of analogs to reinforcement and avoidance. In addition, we agree with earlier reviews that accomplishments or products of behavior are used more frequently as dependent variables than are direct measures of behavior.

ANALYSIS

In the remainder of this article, we will present a detailed analysis of the most salient contingencies in the previously mentioned article by Gaetani et al. (1985). The complexity of these contingencies may be greater than in most of the articles reviewed; and our analysis may be more detailed than would typically be called for. But we offer this as a first approximation to the sort of analysis needed to understand the richness of the behavioral contingencies involved in organizational behavior management.

Natural Contingency

In a high-performance automobile machining shop, two machinists produced billable work at an average of only $88 per day. This was the baseline. As the first step in our conceptual behavioral analysis, let us analyze the natural contingencies in that organization that failed to support an adequate level of productivity:

What was the target behavior? Machining parts at a high rate.

What was the motivating condition before the response? (See the glossary for a distinction between motivating condition and incentive condition.) Before rapidly machining a single part, there was a low probability of a raise or of recognition from the supervisor.

What was the incentive condition after the response? After rapidly machining a single part, the outcome (incentive condition) was a very slightly higher probability of a raise or of recognition from the supervisor. However, those outcomes were cumulative; in other words, if the worker machined enough parts at a high rate, the probability of recognition and of a raise would be substantially higher.

What was the relation between the motivating condition, the response, and the incentive condition? Rapidly machining a single part increased slightly the probability of recognition or a raise.

What was the natural contingency? An ineffective analog to reinforcement. The response produced a slight increase in the probability of a reinforcer. It was not a direct-acting contingency of reinforcement for two reasons: The delay between the response and the reinforcer (recognition or a raise) would most likely have been too great to reinforce the response. (But even when the outcome is delayed, the contingency could be effective or control behavior, if that outcome is sizeable and probable.) And the increment in the probability of the reinforcer was too small to reinforce the response, making this contingency ineffective.

Why was this natural contingency ineffective? Because each instance of rapid machining of a part produced too small an increment in the probability of recognition or of a raise. Only the cumulative effects of each small increment would suffice to cause the supervisor to praise and raise. In other words, the machinists needed to produce at a high rate over a period of days, weeks, or even months, before the supervisor would react; no single instance of rapid machining was of significant value. (Because the contingency was not direct-acting, it would only have controlled the behavior if the behavior had been governed by a rule describing that contingency. However, rules describing contingencies with outcomes [incentive conditions] that are small and of only cumulative significance usually do not control behavior.) See Figure 1 for an analysis of the natural contingency.

Intervention Contingencies

After baseline, Gaetani et al. (1985) set up a commission-based pay-for-performance system of compensation. During the intervention, each machinist received the regular base pay, if the individual billable work equaled baseline rate. In addition, a machinist received a 5% commission on dollars billed above the baseline rate. As a result, average work billed per machinist rose from $88 a day to $254 a day, an increase of 289%. (Incidentally, this 289% increase in productivity resulted from only a 17% increase in pay, an increase from an average of $48 to $56 per day.)

As the second step in our conceptual behavior analysis, let us analyze the intervention contingencies that supported this impressive level of productivity. We will start with what we consider to be perhaps the most crucial but least obvious of those contingencies.

FIGURE 1. Natural contingency: Ineffective analog to reinforcement.

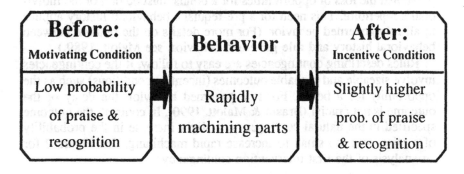

First Intervention Contingency

What was the target behavior? Rapidly machining parts.

What was the motivating condition before the response? Before rapidly machining a particular part, the machinist had the opportunity to earn a bonus for machining future parts during that eight-hour workday. (Whether that opportunity applied to the very next part or later parts depended on whether the machinist had yet reached the baseline level of billable work for that day.)

What was the incentive condition after the response? After rapidly machining the part, the machinist would still have the opportunity to earn a bonus on future parts that day.

What was the relation between the motivating condition, the response, and the incentive condition? Rapid machining maintained the status quo, the opportunity to earn bonuses on future parts.

What was the contingency? An analog to avoidance of the loss of reinforcers, rapid machining of one part avoided the loss of the opportunity to earn bonuses on future parts that day. If the machinist slowed early in the day, he would lose the opportunity for earning a bonus later in the day. The contingency was an analog and not a direct-acting avoidance contingency. This is because the delay between the response and the avoidance of the loss of the reinforcers was too great to reinforce the avoidance response.

Why was this intervention contingency effective? With a high probability, rapid machining avoided the loss of a significant reinforcer (opportunity for a bonus). Because the contingency was not direct-acting, it would only control the behavior indirectly through a rule describing that contingency, for instance, "if I machine rapidly, I will avoid losing the opportunity to earn the bonus." Of course, for this sort of rule to evoke behavior, a pre-requisite behavioral history is required. Responding that prevented the loss of opportunities for a bonus must be part of the individual's repertoire. This need for a pre-requisite behavioral history applies to all rule-governed behavior. (For more details on the relation between behavioral history and rule governed behavior, see Malott, 1989.)

Rules describing contingencies are easy to follow, if the contingencies involve sizeable and probable outcomes (incentive conditions) such as the opportunity for a bonus. For rule-governed behavior, the delay of the outcome is not crucial (Braam & Malott, 1990). In contrast, the outcome specified in the natural contingency, a slight increase in the probability of a raise, was too small to increase rapid machining. See Figure 2 for an analysis of the first intervention contingency.

Second Intervention Contingency

What about the contingency later in the day, after the machinist had exceeded the baseline amount of billable work, when the bonus contingency was now in effect? In other words, what about the bonus contingency itself? We think that by itself, the bonus contingency was not as crucial as it might appear, at first glance; by itself, the bonus contingency might have produced little increase in productivity.

What was the target behavior? Machining a part; but here, in some senses, the rate was not crucial; as long as the machinist finished that part before the end of the workday a reinforcer would be delivered.

What was the motivating condition before the response? Before machining a specific part, the machinist would be due to receive a particular commission (e.g., $6) as a result of having machined the previous three parts.

What was the incentive condition after the response? After machining the part, the outcome was a significantly higher commission (e.g., $8).

What was the relation between the motivating condition, the response, and the incentive condition? Machining each part significantly increased the commission.

What was the contingency? An analog to reinforcement. The response produced a significant reinforcer (e.g., $2) with a high probability. However, it was not a direct-acting contingency because the delay between the response and the reinforcer was too great to produce reinforcement.

Why was this intervention contingency effective? Here is an obvious answer: After the machinist reached the day's baseline production, each further part completed produced a significant outcome or incentive, bonus. (Because the contingency was not direct-acting, it would only control the behavior if the behavior were governed by a rule describing that

FIGURE 2. First intervention contingency: Analog to avoidance.

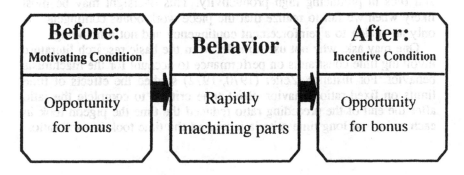

contingency. And rules describing contingencies with sizeable and probable outcomes [incentive conditions] do control behavior, even if the outcome is delayed.) But we think this obvious answer may be wrong; so let us look at another contingency.

Deadline–The end of the workday constituted a deadline or limited hold. When the eight-hour day was up, the machinists would no longer earn bonuses for that day. Also, they could not earn bonuses on the next several parts they machined during the early hours of the next workday (first they would have to reach their goal of billable work). Deadlines such as this may generally establish indirect-acting analogs to avoidance contingencies. And analog avoidance contingencies may be crucial to the maintenance of high rates of production.

For contrast, imagine that there had been no deadline. Imagine, instead, that the machinists earned a bonus for each part completed. Further imagine that they could work on this bonus piece-rate basis as many hours a day as they wished and there were no impatient spouse or demanding creditor imposing deadlines external to the work setting. Procrastination would soon rear its ugly head, especially with indirect-acting contingencies delivering delayed reinforcers (bonuses), and even more especially when those reinforcers are learned reinforcers (dollars) that might not be exchanged immediately for backup reinforcers (e.g., food). Under such conditions, each minute off task would cost the machinist very little. It would be only after a day of accumulating many minutes off task that procrastination's price would become significant; and even then, the lost opportunity to earn bonuses earlier in the day would be a sunk cost; so one more minute on a cigarette break still would have only the smallest of aversive effects on the day's earnings. In other words, one minute's rapid working would not avoid a sufficiently sizeable loss of reinforcers. So the avoidance of the loss of reinforcers would not compete with the reinforcers of the cigarette break.

We often fail to appreciate the importance of the aversive control of deadline-induced avoidance contingencies in preventing procrastination and thus in producing high productivity. This oversight may be most likely when we fail to realize that the piece-work bonus contingency is only an analog to a reinforcement contingency and not a homolog.

One may ask, why not use a model from the basic research literature involving time constraints on performance to account for the machinists behavior. For instance, Zeiler (1970, 1972) studied the effects of time limits on fixed-ratio behavior. Brief time criteria to complete the ratio after the end of the preceding ratio reduced the time the pigeon took in each ratio; and long time criteria increased the time took in each ratio.

We believe there are fundamental differences between the conditions controlling the behavior of the pigeon in Zieler's (1970, 1972) studies and those controlling the behavior of the worker in Gaetani's (1985) study; and such differences do not permit a simple comparison. First, the worker is not a pigeon deprived of food for 23 hours, and maintained at 80% of its free-feeding weight when exposed to the intervention contingencies.

Second, the worker's behavior does not get reinforced with the unlearned reinforcer of food immediately following each response or even the terminal response at the end of each ratio. Instead, the worker will receive the outcome (the bonus) about a week after the occurrence of each specific behavior. To shift the metaphor, unlike the squirrel, we tend to put off the collection of our nuts for a distant winter's day, in a manner much different from the way we rapidly crack those nuts and hastily eat them, if we have been food deprived for a few hours. Only when we are actually cracking and eating the nuts would our behavior be under the control of a direct-acting contingency of reinforcement like the one controlling the diligent behavior of the rat in the animal laboratory. And only in that case would the deadline-induced avoidance contingency be superfluous. In the case of the machinists, we suggest the deadline is far from superfluous; instead it is crucial to the effectiveness of the bonus contingency.

Furthermore, when we are dealing with human beings and there is considerable delay between the response and the outcome, as with the machinists, we cannot ignore that verbal behavior plays a critical role. In other words, we do not need to address rule-governed behavior to account for the pigeon's performance; but we must do so to account for the machinists'.

So what is wrong with the obvious answer to why the bonus contingency was effective, to the answer that the bonus contingency was an indirect-acting analog to reinforcement because it produced probable, sizeable outcomes? We think that, by itself, the bonus contingency would not be effective (that was the point of our asking you to imagine what it would be like without some sort of implicit deadline). The outcome of each minute of work was not sufficiently sizeable to support compliance with the rule describing that contingency.

Here is our answer to why the bonus contingency was effective. It was effective because it combined with (a) an implicit deadline and with (b) the first intervention contingency (an analog to avoidance of the opportunity to earn bonuses on future parts that day). Rapid machining produced a bonus for each part completed, but more importantly, it constantly avoided the loss of the opportunity to earn maximal or optimal bonuses for that day, no room for procrastination. The complex contingency was effective only because the worker could state the rule, "If I do not stop putting off and start producing, I will not have a chance to earn enough of a bonus by the end of the workday." See Figure 3 for an analysis of the second intervention contingency.

Theoretical Contingency

The main point of our analysis is that most contingencies constituting the culture of an organization and most interventions of an organizational behavior manager are indirect-acting rule-governed analogs to direct-acting contingencies of reinforcement (including presentation of reinforcers, escape, and avoidance) and punishment (usually penalty). The question remains, how does the statement of the relevant rules govern organizational behavior? Our answer is that rules govern behavior by establishing direct-acting contingencies of reinforcement and punishment (Malott, 1984, 1988, 1989, 1991; Malott & Malott, 1991).

As the final question in our conceptual behavior analysis of machinist contingencies, let us ask, what were the theoretical direct-acting contingencies that might have supported the indirect-acting intervention contingencies? We will consider only the analog to avoidance of the loss of reinforcers. The rapid machining early in the day avoided the loss of the opportunity to earn bonuses later in the day. (The bonus contingency, combined with the implicit deadlines, was so intimately involved with the avoidance contingency that a separate analysis would add nothing new.) The contingency was an analog and not a direct-acting avoidance contingency, because of the long delay between the response and the time when the loss of the reinforcer would be avoided.

FIGURE 3. Second intervention contingency: Analog to reinforcement.

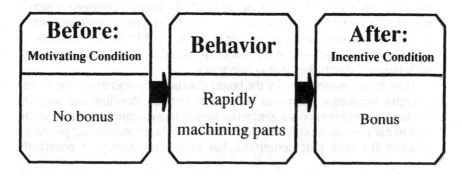

What was the target behavior? Machining at a high rate.

What was the motivating condition before the response? The machinist was in a slightly aversive condition of "fear" or "anxiety" because he might lose the opportunity to earn bonuses.

What was the establishing operation for that motivating condition? Stating the rule describing the bonus contingency established not rapidly machining a part as an aversive condition. For example, every time a machinist took a coffee break, he was in a condition that could cost him the opportunity to earn the day's bonuses. A statement of the rule established noncompliance with that rule as an aversive condition. But rule statements generate aversive conditions, only if the individual has a relevant behavioral history and repertoire (Malott, 1989). For instance, the rule, "I would better get back to work, or I might lose the opportunity for a bonus," might not generate an aversive condition ("fear" or "anxiety") without a history of having lost rewards because of noncompliance with rules.

What was the incentive condition after the response? The response class consisted of the acts of machining at a high rate. As long as the machinist worked rapidly and productively, he escaped and stayed out of the maximally aversive condition of noncompliance with the rule (e.g., the condition of "anxiety" or "fear"). However, the incentive condition resulting from high-rate work may still have been a little aversive but not as much as when the machinist was off task or working at a low rate.

What was the relation between the motivating condition, the response, and the incentive condition? Rapid machining immediately escaped or reduced the aversive motivating condition of "fear" of the loss of the opportunity for bonuses and put the machinist in a less aversive incentive condition where there was less "fear" of that loss.

What was the contingency? A direct-acting escape contingency.

Why was this inferred, theoretical contingency effective? Because its outcome (the incentive condition) was immediate, probable, and sizeable.

See Figure 4 for an analysis of the theoretical contingency.

CONCLUSIONS

Researchers in organizational behavior management have made great practical contributions by developing a technology for the management of the performance of employees so that their performance is in keeping with the culture and goals of the organization. Now behavior analysis may have reached a level of maturity and sophistication that will allow

FIGURE 4. Theoretical contingency: Escape.

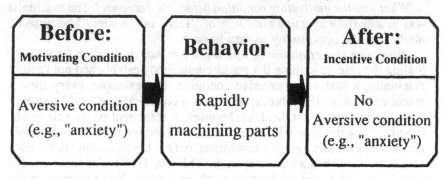

these researchers to enhance their contributions to the theory and science of behavior as well as to the practical concerns of the organization. Now researchers might include in their experimental reports theoretical analyses of the ineffective natural contingencies that necessitated their intervention, the indirect and direct-acting intervention contingencies, and the inferred direct-acting contingencies that supported the indirect-acting intervention contingencies. We do not present our current analyses as the final word, just the latest. No doubt, as we and other behavior analysts ponder in increasing depth the natural and added contingencies in organizational cultures, the resulting analyses will gain in sophistication and validity. It may be that we or others will develop better analysis even of the study considered in the present article. At best, we view our current efforts as one more step toward a greater understanding of organizational culture and organizational behavior management. Our goal is to encourage organizational behavior managers to give more thought to the behavioral processes underlying their interventions and to share those thoughts with the readers of their research reports, thus contributing to the theory and science of behavior analysis as well as to its technology.

GLOSSARY

Contingency. A response, an outcome, and a stimulus in the presence of which the outcome is contingent on that response.
Direct-acting contingency. A contingency for which the outcome is sufficiently large, probable, and immediate to reinforce or punish the response.

Incentive condition. The value (size, intensity, etc.) of the reinforcer or aversive condition that follows a response. In an analysis of behavioral contingencies, the motivating condition is the state of the organism or its environment immediately before the response; and the incentive condition is that state immediately after the response. For example, the motivating condition might be dehydration, the response might be drinking water, and the incentive condition might be less dehydration. Or the motivating condition might be 4 ma of electricity on the rat's shock grid, the response might be lever pressing, and the incentive condition might be 0 ma of shock.

Indirect-acting contingency. An effective contingency for which the outcome is too delayed to reinforce or punish the response.

Ineffective contingency. A contingency that does not control behavior, often because the outcome is too improbable or too small, even though the outcome may be of cumulative significance.

Limited hold. Reinforcement is available for only a limited time.

Motivating condition. The condition of an organism's body or environment that directly affects the sensitivity of that organism's behavior (a) to reinforcement or punishment by particular reinforcing or aversive conditions and (b) to evocation or suppression by associated discriminative stimuli.

Natural contingencies. The contingencies operative prior to the intervention.

Rule. A verbal description of a contingency.

Rule-governed behavior. Behavior controlled by the statement of a rule rather than by reinforcement or punishment of the behavior in the contingency the rule describes.

REFERENCES

Balcazar, F. E., Shupert, M. K., Daniels, A. C., Mawhinney, T. C., & Hopkins, B. L. (1989). An objective review and analysis of ten years of publication in the *Journal of Organizational Behavior Management*. *Journal of Organizational Behavior Management, 10*, 7-37.

Braam, C., & Malott, R. W. (1990). "I'll do it when the snow melts": The effects of deadlines and delayed outcomes on rule-governed behavior in preschool children. *The Analysis of Verbal Behavior, 8*, 67-76.

Brown, K. M., Willis, B. S., & Reid, D. H. (1981). Differential effects of supervisor verbal feedback and feedback plus approval on institutional staff performance. *Journal of Organizational Behavior Management, 3*, 57-68.

Crowell, C. R., Anderson, D. C., Abel, D. M., & Sergio, J. P. (1988). Task clarification, performance feedback, and social praise: Procedures for improving the customer service of bank tellers. *Journal of Applied Behavior Analysis, 21,* 65-71.

Gaetani, J. J., Hoxeng, D. D., & Austin, J. T. (1985). Engineering compensation systems: Effects of commissioned versus wage payment. *Journal of Organizational Behavior Management, 7,* 51-63.

Frost, J. M., Hopkins, B. L., & Conard, R. J. (1981). An analysis of the effects of feedback and reinforcement on machine-paced production. *Journal of Organizational Behavior Management, 3,* 5-18.

Kello, J. E., Geller, E. S., Rice, J. C., & Bryant, S. L. (1988). Motivating auto safety belt wearing in industrial settings: From awareness to behavior change. *Journal of Organizational Behavior Management, 9,* 7-21.

Malott, R. W. (1984). Rule-governed behavior, self-management, and the developmentally disabled: A theoretical analysis. *Analysis and Intervention in Developmental Disabilities, 4,* 199-209.

Malott, R. W. (1988). Rule-governed behavior and behavioral anthropology. *The Behavior Analyst, 11,* 181-203.

Malott, R. W. (1989). The achievement of evasive goals: Control by rules describing contingencies that are not direct acting. In S. C. Hayes (Ed.), *Rule-governed behavior: Cognition, contingencies, and instructional control* (pp. 269-322). New York: Plenum.

Malott, R. W. (1992). Rule-governed behavior and organizational behavior management: The theory. *Journal of Organizational Behavior Management, 12* (2).

Malott, R. W., & Malott, M. E. (1991). Private events and rule-governed behavior. In L. J. Hayes & P. N. Chase (Eds.), *Dialogues on verbal behavior* (pp. 237-257). Reno, NV: Context Press.

Merwin, G. A., Jr., Thomason, J. A., & Sanford, E. E. (1989). A methodology and content review of organizational behavior management in the private sector: 1978-1986. *Journal of Organizational Behavior Management, 10,* 39-57.

Newby, T. J., & Robinson, P. W. (1983). Effects of grouped and individual feedback and reinforcement on retail employee performance. *Journal of Organizational Behavior Management, 5,* 51-68.

Zeiler, M. D. (1970). Time limits for completing fixed ratios. *Journal of the Experimental Analysis of Behavior, 14,* 275-286.

Zeiler, M. D. (1972). Time limits for completing fixed ratios. II. Stimulus specificity. *Journal of the Experimental Analysis of Behavior, 18,* 243-251.

Organizational Behavior Management Within Structural and Cultural Constraints: An Example from the Human Service Sector

Beth Sulzer-Azaroff
Martin J. Pollack
Richard K. Fleming

SUMMARY. In human service settings, as in all organizations, performance management is best accomplished by arranging contingencies to enhance wanted and diminish unwanted behavior. However, managers need to avoid presuming that one set of contingencies will work equivalently well across varied organizations. One reason is that the potential reinforcers inherent within the formal structure and culture of one system may not be present in the next. Recognizing this fact is critical because selecting reinforcers indigenous to the system impacts on generalization and long term maintenance. In that regard, human service settings pose special challenges, as often they lack ready access to the many of the reinforcers naturally available elsewhere. To illustrate the differences that might exist within the network of contingencies between two classes of establishments, hypothetical organizational charts are displayed and discussed, one for a private industry; the other for a

Beth Sulzer-Azaroff is affiliated with the University of Massachusetts, Amherst. Martin J. Pollack is affiliated with Southbury Training School. Richard K. Fleming is associated with Auburn University.

This paper is based on an invited address presented at the Florida Association for Behavior Analysis, Organizational Behavior Managements Network, Clearwater Beach, FL, January, 1991.

Requests for reprints should be directed to: Beth Sulzer-Azaroff, Department of Psychology, University of Massachusetts, Amherst, MA 01003.

non-profit human service agency. An analysis of each network of formal and informal contingencies suggests those that might be managed with greater or lesser success. Case examples from the two types of organizations are provided to illustrate these distinctions. By carefully examining the common and unique factors influencing employees' performance within a given type, managers should be able to design more effective and durable programs of change.

ORGANIZATIONAL BEHAVIOR MANAGEMENT IN HUMAN SERVICE SETTINGS

Regardless of the type of organization involved, performance is likely to improve when carefully selected target behaviors are defined and contingencies identified, analyzed and effectively managed. To automatically transfer a set of practices from one system to another would be a mistake because the extent to which any given intervention might succeed probably depends upon the distinctive features of the specific organization involved (Mawhinney, in press). Each enterprise is unique in terms of the interplay of contingencies operating within its system and the opportunities available for altering those contingencies. Especially critical is identifying the reinforcers indigenous to a particular setting because harnessing those that are readily available bodes well for generalization and long term maintenance (Stokes & Baer, 1977).

Nevertheless, the assessment process might be expedited by recognizing that some identifiable commonalities exist within organizational classes that do not occur among organizations belonging to distinctly different organizational classes. For instance, private industries often share a concern with factors that influence profits, while human service organizations tend to emphasize quality of care. Other important contingencies including, in particular, those embedded within the organization's culture also simultaneously are at play. As with any other situation in which multiple schedules are operating, these various contingencies may restrict or enhance the results of planned interventions. Recognizing those between class differences and within class commonalities should help performance managers plan and execute their programs more effectively and efficiently by guiding their selection of specific strategies.

The perspective just discussed characterizes "behavioral systems analysis" (Krapfl & Gasparotto, 1982). "Behavioral systems analysis is a blend of behavior analysis and systems analysis perspectives in that the environment of interest for the behavioral systems analyst is generally a complex environment . . . and the behavior of interest is that which is controlled by that organizational environment" (p. 24).

In behavioral systems analysis, the network of operating contingencies within the organization is examined to see where the supports and impediments to change may lie. Included would be the formally structured network of contingencies along with the more subtle influences at work. So in addition to the more apparent reinforcers like salaries and benefits, to a greater or lesser degree, other elements affect the performance of individuals within the system: the nature of the job, job security, products or results of job performance, opportunity for promotion and to acquire new skills, support services, available supplies and equipment, physical surroundings, laws, public and organizational policies, the vagaries of the market place, unions, pressure and potential take-over groups, media, reactions of family or family surrogates and peers, external funding and individual histories and current setting events and establishing operations and many others. While each individual member of an organization differs in response to those combined influences, here we are interested in the general effects within different classes of organizations.

The purpose of this paper is to examine some of the distinctive features of the network of contingencies frequently operating in human service settings and contrast them with those often encountered in the private sector. First we will look at two hypothetical organizational charts to which have been added a number of informal sources of supports and impediments. Then we shall discuss the implications of those spheres of influence from a behavior systems analytic perspective, offering case illustrations drawn from our own past experiences. Finally, we shall attempt to identify those distinctive elements that tend to be shared across human service settings in order to help performance managers to initiate planning of successful strategies within those kinds of organizations.

PRIVATE INDUSTRY

As a point of departure, sources of formal and informal contingencies operating in a hypothetical manufacturing plant are depicted in Figure 1. For the sake of simplicity, the manufacturing jobs of just a few production units are illustrated. The solid boxes enclose aspects of the formal operation, while those with dashed perimeters represent other potential sources of support or impediments to progress.

With the input of managerial and administrative associates, the chief executive officer carries out the policies established by the Board of Directors. Those actions are mediated by various other upper level and middle managers, who, depending on the power of the union(s), control

FIGURE 1. Organizational chart for a hypothetical private industry. Solid lines indicate formally designed control over contingencies. Dashed lines show contingencies not formally structured.

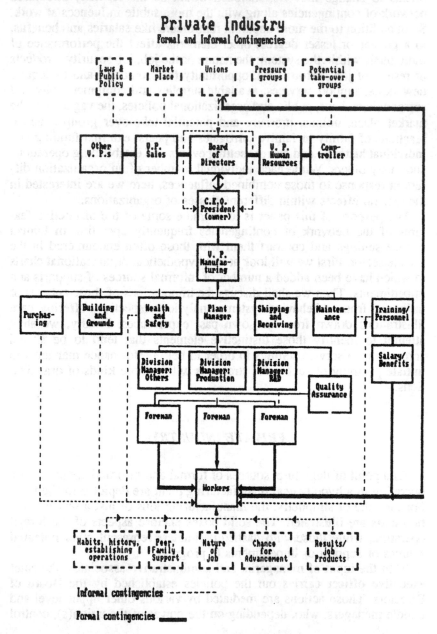

Private Industry
Formal and Informal Contingencies

Informal contingencies ------

Formal contingencies _____

wages, increments, benefits, schedules, job assignments and recognition. Although presumably the Board is free to set policy, numerous outside groups exert pressure. Laws relative to working conditions, plant conditions, chemical emissions and so on exert a strong influence, usually in the form of negative reinforcement (avoiding fines or litigation). These combine with market factors, such as supply, demand and fluctuating stock value plus union and other sources of pressure and hovering hostile take-over groups (again negative reinforcers).

Viewing the factors influencing the workers who do the actual production job, it can be seen that beyond the contingencies already mentioned, other formal and informal contingencies exist (Mawhinney and Ford, 1977; Mawhinney, 1979): Job training; feedback from quality assurance personnel; approval or disapproval expressed by friends and family; the enjoyment intrinsic to the job; the products generated; opportunities for advancement or reassignment; and many others. While many of the latter are shared across workers, unique are individual learning histories and antecedents, including setting events (e.g., assignments, instructions) and establishing operations (health status, recent interpersonal conflicts and so on) that affect the moment to moment performance of each employee.

What does an analysis of this type tell us? It directs us to identify how optimally these contingencies are currently operating and how they might be further harnessed toward supporting change. The information reminds us for instance, that some consequences are inefficient reinforcers because they are delayed, negative, infrequent, and may be of little value (of inappropriate quality) to the worker (Agnew & Redmon, 1992; Malott, 1992; Malott, Shimamune, & Malott, 1992).

Consider number of rejects identified by quality assurance. Workers may not suffer loss of any major reinforcers when the goods they produce fail to meet standards of quality. Any negative feedback they receive tends to be delayed and inconsistent (Mawhinney, 1986; Notz, Boschman, & Tax, 1987). Producing goods conforming to quality standards is ignored in many organizations, so why would good quality matter to them? (This is not to say that all organizations exhibit indifference to quality and individual consequences for its maintenance (for examples see Handlin (in press) and Zemke & Gunkler (1982)). The same sort of analysis can be conducted for just about any set of elements within the network.

In fact, in many standard manufacturing operations like the one depicted here, only a few reinforcing contingencies appear to be functioning at optimal levels (i.e., discriminable, positive, immediate, consistent, and of appropriate quality and in sufficient quantity): The job process or result;

enthusiastic attention from supervisors, peers or oneself; and, in piece work, the number of items produced. Wages, benefits, raises, favorable performance reviews, formal recognition, promotions, preferred assignments and other rewards fail the criteria for optimal effectiveness because they usually are not directly contingent on performance, and tend to be delayed or too irregular, improbable, or not "valued by" (i.e., reinforcing or functional for) the worker at that time.

As organizational behavior management has repeatedly shown, however, other sources can be harnessed: Modifying the pay structure so it becomes more directly contingent upon performance (e.g., George & Hopkins, 1989; Luthans, Paul & Taylor, 1985); adjusting the timing and types of feedback messages delivered by supervisors (e.g., Crowell, Anderson, Abel, & Sergio, 1988; see also Balcazar, Shupert, Daniels, Mawhinney & Hopkins, 1989 for a review), peers (Sulzer-Azaroff, Fox, Moss & Davis, 1987) and workers themselves (Kissel, Whitman & Reid, 1983; Komaki, Blood & Holder, 1980); treating operations that establish events antithetical to effective productivity, such as stress, via stress management programs (see the *Journal of Organizational Behavior Management*, volume 8 (2), 1986) and so on. Interfering contingencies, like those spawned by dissatisfaction with the nature of the job also may be adjusted. Examples are job diversification, reassignment or rearrangement of organizational structure (Frederiksen, Riley & Myers, 1984).

Recognizing existing but immutable contingencies also helps, because efforts will not be wasted where payoff is impossible. For instance, the union contract may not permit adjustments in compensation, although a benefit such as an awards banquet or opportunity to learn a new skill may be permitted. These sorts of strategies are familiar to practitioners of organizational behavior management: pay-for-performance, supervisory feedback, goal setting, social reinforcement schemes and numerous others.

Hooking onto existing reinforcers or putting supports in place on an organization-wide basis illustrates effective organizational contingency management at work. (Developing a completely organization-wide intervention is another matter (for an example see Zemke & Gunkler, 1982).) The hooking on and adding supports strategy was exemplified in a successful safety program developed at a telecommunications plant (Sulzer-Azaroff, Loafman, Merante & Hlavacek, 1990). Numerous elements of the operation were harnessed to support safer performance by workers on the job. Beginning with the Chief Executive Officer at the plant, whose own management incentive plan included a provision for a reduction in accidents, supervisors and specialized personnel, including the safety department, recognized the same goal as an important aspect of their acceptable job performance. That helped everyone to work toward the identical end: the safety department to cooperate in designing and conducting a valid auditing program; managers, who participated in publicly recognizing accomplishments; the photographic department, who produced and updated large attractive graphs; foremen, who conducted their own informal audits, repaired potential hazardous conditions, suggested redesigns of jobs, coordinated review, reinforcement and goal-setting meetings with the workers; and the workers themselves, who suggested ways to improve safety on the job and reinforcers when sub-goals and final goals ultimately were met. In one case, even the worker's children involved themselves by viewing a video tape of their mother performing a wire wrap job and suggesting ways for her to diminish her superfluous repetitive motions.

By contrast, we avoided blind alleys by analyzing the system's history in terms of occupational accidents. Recognizing that intervening in some areas would have little payoff, we addressed the plant's "hot-spots." Little effort was wasted in attempting to dispense reinforcers, such as cash incentives or time off, because their delivery would not be condoned by various units within and outside of the organization. (One impediment we failed to predict was the recent sale of the plant. Whether that has led to an adverse realignment of the contingency network is not possible to determine.)

Certainly, the manipulable contingencies at different levels in for-profit industrial organizations vary, as do the potential new sources to harness toward improving performance. For instance, union contracts may obviate using various forms of compensation as reinforcers. Yet, regardless of any organization's explicit system of compensation, usually industrial and business firms do maintain a good deal of internal control over many reinforcers. By contrast, when the public service sector is involved, as often is the case in human services, contingency control tends to be more external to the specific organization, thereby further challenging effective management. Other distinctive features are at play as well in human service settings.

HUMAN SERVICE ORGANIZATIONS

Special problems present themselves in the human service setting for a variety of reasons. At the most basic level is deciding what performances to target for change. Global, philosophical goals commonly predominate, with the result that specific purposes of the program and the job tasks of the contributors tend to be amorphous and often lack clear accountabilities. In publicly supported service agencies, explicit reinforcing contingencies, such as salaries and benefits, usually are delivered according to fixed time rather than fixed ratio schedules (staff are paid regularly regardless of specific accomplishments) and both explicit and implicit reinforcers (promotions, assignments, recognition and so on) frequently are controlled by governmental bureaucracies. Typically, the network of contingencies is arranged and it functions differently from that of private industry. Examining the distinctive elements of a particular human service setting, however, can prove just as productive as with any other organization.

Consider Figure 2, which is analogous to Figure 1, but designed to depict a hypothetical non-profit human service agency. An analysis of this organization's contingency network indicates a number of external forces that powerfully impact the system and highlights problems arising from conflicting or ambiguous lines of authority depicted in the diagram.

Notice how salaries and benefits are set outside of the organization. (So are job classification and selection schemes.) As a political appointee, the commissioner's expertise in the area of developmental disabilities may vary. Added to the commissioner's direct influence on the chief administrator of the local agency are numerous external sources of positive and negative reinforcement: the media (that thrive on the sensational in human interest realm); numerous federal, state, local, and departmental regulations, policies, decrees; the state of the economy; availability of and eligibility for grants and direct reimbursement for meeting standards of treatment or quality of care; groups that exert pressure, such as parents, client advocates, business and real estate interests, tax reform groups, unions, and others. Responding to negative pressure from those sources can be extremely negatively reinforcing because the action terminates the ongoing, often highly aversive stimulation.

The actions motivated by external forces are not always antithetical to the agency's mission, though. Everyone has witnessed instances of improved quality of treatment resulting from press exposes, litigation or pressure groups. On a local level, one instance was an agency's decision to undertake a major program to improve employee safety after a series of news reports highlighted the soaring rates of staff injuries and the resultant cost to the tax payers.

Typically though, reactions to aversive outside pressures tend to sap valuable human and material resources, impeding fulfillment of the mission of the organization. Among examples we have seen in various hu-

FIGURE 2. Organizational chart for a hypothetical non-profit publicly supported human service agency. Solid lines indicate formally designed control over contingencies. Dashed lines show contingencies not formally structured.

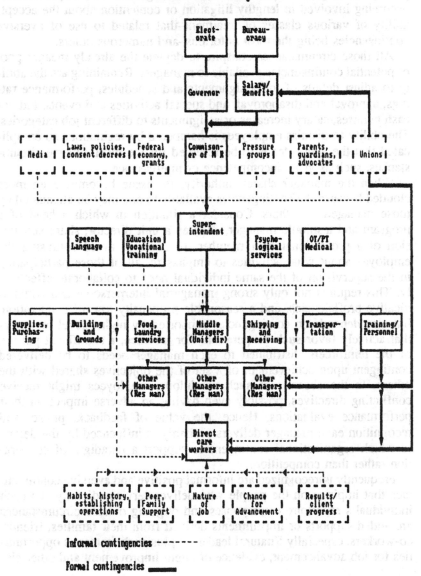

Non-profit Human Service Agency
Formal and Informal Contingencies

Informal contingencies `-------`

Formal contingencies `_____`

man service agencies have been: sacrificing scarce resources that could be better spent on services to clients in order to make the surroundings look more pleasing to visitors; preparing extensive paper plans without any accompanying action (e.g., X Individual Service Plans designed, perhaps of insignificant value or without being effectively implemented); becoming involved in lengthy litigation or contention about the acceptability of various classes of treatment–that related to use of aversive contingencies being the most notorious–and numerous others.

All those circumstances conspire to deplete the already meager pool of potential contingencies available to managers. Remaining are the ability to adjust details of job assignments and schedules, performance ratings, approval and disapproval, and special activities and events; but not cash bonuses, salary increases or assignments to different job categories. The ability to dismiss employees is hampered by regulations so complicated that the action tends to be reserved for the most adverse circumstances, such as gross incompetence or malfeasance.

When the manager shares authority, the issue becomes even more clouded because the contingencies available to one may be attenuated by those managed by others. Consider a situation in which a head of a program and a middle manager, such as a unit director, share supervision of a professional staff member. In order to avoid confusing the employee about what activities to emphasize, all of those participating in the supervision of the same individual need to collaborate effectively. This requires not only strong managerial interpersonal and communicative proficiencies, and a reasonable propensity toward cooperation, but also depends on contingencies supported by higher level managers that actively favor such cooperation. For instance, a significant portion of the reinforcers distributed to each manager needs to be delivered contingent upon achievement of a set of the objectives shared with the others. In the absence of such conditions, employees might receive conflicting directives, possibly even having an adverse impact on their performance evaluations. Hence, the value of feedback, praise, and recognition each manager delivers probably is influenced by the degree to which organizational contingencies support a paradigm of cooperation rather than competition.

Frequently unrecognized are informal positive and aversive contingencies that impinge on the people who deliver services directly. To each individual's repertoire of responses and ongoing outside circumstances are added supports or impediments derived from their families, friends, co-workers, especially "natural leaders," plus such factors as opportunities for job advancement, evidence of client improvement and other elements of the organizational culture. In contrast with the more formal ones, such informal factors may actually exert greater control over the employee's daily activities because they may happen frequently and immediately contingent on certain actions. Peer influence is a good example. Peers generally are present and their approval or disapproval can be very influential, especially in the sense that actions by co-workers can make job conditions more or less tolerable on a moment-to-moment basis (Mawhinney & Gowen, 1990).

Recently, we informally surveyed members of an audience of about 50 organizational behavior managers employed, in roughly even proportions, either in industry and in human services. All were asked to indicate the factors they believed influenced their own job performance most heavily. For those in industry, their own learning history, the nature of the job, benefits and bonuses, salary and family factors were said to be most powerful. Those in service agencies reported that the nature of the job, public media, their families and their own learning histories exerted the greatest influence. Notice that the former made no mention of the public media, while latter group failed to emphasize benefits or wages. Clearly, they perceived different contingencies at work. The fallacy of assuming that managing the same set of contingencies will work with equivalent effectiveness, regardless of the nature of the organization, is apparent. Adjustments must be made according to the contingencies common to particular classes of organizations as well as to those unique to any particular setting. Let us illustrate further by showing how this approach was put to profitable use in a human service agency.

A CASE EXAMPLE

Three years ago, a Performance Management (PM) System was to be introduced among the staff of the psychology department in a residential facility for the developmentally disabled. The challenge was distinct because, as often is the case with service providers, job descriptions and functions tended to be ambiguous. The forty participants held bachelors, masters, or doctoral degrees and represented a breadth of experience in the field and in the institution. Some were relative neophytes, while others had been on the staff for many years. As in most such situations, state job requirements were specified as generic processes (e.g., to conduct assessments, offer counseling and so on). Historically, management practices primarily consisted of negatively consequating unacceptable performance, such as failing to complete specific assignments in a timely manner.

By contrast, the PM system was designed to focus on, support and recognize quantitative and qualitative *progress* in staff performance over time. Preplanning with the director of the psychological services program, and with top and middle level agency managers included reviewing the organizational lines of authority, the agency mission and objectives, ongoing accountability and data systems and formal and informal contingency networks. Subsequently, all efforts were directed toward supporting accomplishment of organizational goals.

Building on existing functional groupings–a unit management system was in place–four groups of approximately ten members each was organized. Each group participated in a series of workshops, also initially attended by its unit directors (who were not members of the psychology department) while pinpoints were being selected. (Topics for the workshops are listed on Table 1.) Under the authors' supervision, during intervals of one to four weeks between workshop sessions, participants began to implement each new PM component. Additional consultation was provided by two graduate students of organizational behavior management.

Presented as a system to be instituted permanently, rather than as just another in-service training program, PM was incorporated within the regular management structure. It persists today, although the groupings have been modified in response to changes within the system. Twice monthly, each group assembles with the program director to rapidly review graphs of individual and group accomplishments. Deserved commendations are delivered and individual objectives or "pinpoints" and group goals set for the next session. Selecting those pinpoints that are apparently directed toward efficiently and effectively fulfilling the mission of the institution, the aims of the psychology department, and of the

Table 1

Workshop Topics

1. Overview and objectives

2. Setting pinpoints

3. Measurement and recording

4. Graphing

5. Reinforcement, Feedback & Goal Setting

6. Presenting programs

7. Maintaining performance

unit with which the staff member is affiliated, is selectively praised and acknowledged in other positive ways. So are choosing challenging but attainable long and short term goals and showing evidence of progress toward achieving them. Following the Director's lead, peers now often are the main purveyors of such recognition. Letters to participants and/or supervisors commenting on accomplishments and other rewards occasionally are delivered for especially meritorious performance.

What outcomes have resulted from these efforts? Several. First, over time, participants have learned to set more realistic goals–that is, the number of goals they achieved more and more closely matched those they had set during the semi-monthly sessions (see Figure 3).

Second, the quality of pinpoints has gradually shifted toward more complex and substantive departmental and organizational goals. New targets often reflect the priorities emphasized in related professional development sessions. Table 2 illustrates some sample pinpoints at the outset and some after the system had been in effect for six months. The latter can be characterized as more innovative, challenging and proactive.

As one example, assessments aimed at isolating the function of the self abuse or aggression of clients designated "at risk" have increased considerably (Figure 4). The advantage of such assessments is that they are directed toward *solving* rather than simply controlling those difficulties. Notice that in June, before the importance of these forms of assessment had been emphasized in the performance management meetings, only 61% of the clients' maladaptive behaviors had been assessed for their function, while afterward that number rose to 94%. Simultaneously, in June, although 80% of the clients had behavior management programs designed for them, presumably at least 19% of those must have been conceived without data related to function. Ten months later, 97% had programs that in almost all cases, incorporated findings from the functional assessments.

Initial staff apprehensions have been largely overcome. Most participants have embraced the process as a mechanism for sharing their accomplishments and learning about their peers' responses to challenging professional problems. They appear to enjoy seeing evidence of and receiving peer and supervisory recognition for their achievements.

While not an unqualified success (a few participants still grouse at having to plan and account for their accomplishments regularly), the system has continued to flourish for over two years, to the increasing benefit of staff and clients alike. In contrast with the typically transitory improvement seen with in-service training programs, PM continues. What are some of the possible explanations?

Presumably, the value of analyzing the formal and informal network

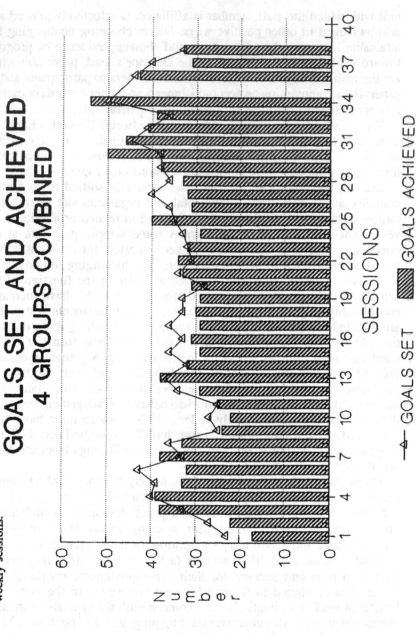

FIGURE 3. Number of goals set and achieved by all forty members of the Psychology Department over 38 bi-weekly sessions.

Table 2

Illustrative Pinpoints

At Outset

Completing routine evaluations on time

Increasing time spent in client residences; day services
programs

Encouraging staff attendance at "community meetings".

Developing new pinpoints

Holding in-service training sessions

After Six Months

Completing behavioral assessments

Writing and implementing treatment programs

Preparing video vignettes for in-service training

Preparing and delivering training program in generic skills for
staff

Designing and presenting social skills, communication
skills, sex education training programs to clients

Training staff how to interact with clients

Increasing participation by staff in meetings

Tracking and analyzing time spent by professionals and
assignments accomplished

Reading professional articles

Completing redesign of data systems

of contingencies has proved advantageous in our attempts to implement effective programming among human service professionals. Here is how the meager pool of available formal contingencies was augmented by those readily accessible within the system:

• Attendance at the initial training sessions was reinforced with snacks (and presumably reasonably appealing content and process)

- Having familiarized ourselves with the institutions' missions and annual goals, we made every attempt to tie pinpoints to them. Accordingly, the professionals' activities were valued by their supervisors and annual performance ratings began to reflect successful and noteworthy pinpoints.
- To obtain their support, Unit Directors helped guide the initial selection of pinpoints by the psychological service personnel assigned to their units.
- Peer support was garnered by modeling and prompting it (e.g., "What do you especially like about that pinpoint?") and by applying feedback and recognition for group as well as for individual progress.
- Recognition and approval from managers was achieved by inviting them periodically to attend training and later feedback-reinforcement and goal-setting sessions and by notifying them about special individual accomplishments.
- Recognition from other sources was obtained by some who were encouraged to present their pinpointed projects at meetings and conferences. For example, one professional gave a well received workshop on her staff training program at a regional conference on developmental disabilities. Two others presented posters at a special Parent's Day hosted by one of the units.
- A reinforcer survey (Figure 5) revealed other available items or events that might be meaningfully delivered contingent upon goal attainment. (Interestingly, the social reinforcers tended to receive the strongest endorsement. As might be expected, individual differences emerged. Some people identified and received extra clinical supervision as a consequence of their progress with their pinpoints. Others, who received requested letters of recognition, not only expressed their satisfaction with that consequence, but vigorously began to increase the number of goals they identified and accomplished.)

In other programs set in human service settings, we have formally involved peers (Fleming & Sulzer-Azaroff, 1991), and either direct supervisors or non-supervisory experts (Fox & Sulzer-Azaroff, 1989) in the delivery of feedback. Feedback about results when added to process feedback also appeared to help sustain nurses' delivery of feedback to their assistants (Babcock, Sulzer-Azaroff, & Sanderson, 1989). Of course, numerous other examples of use of performance feedback, goal-setting and reinforcement in human service settings can be found in the OBM literature (see Balcazar, Hopkins & Suarez, 1985/86). Not generally rep-

FIGURE 4. Behavioral assessments and behavioral programs developed for "at risk" clients during June, prior to an emphasis on functional assessments during PM meetings and after that focus had been introduced.

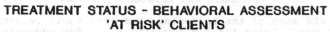

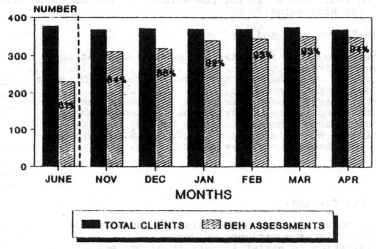

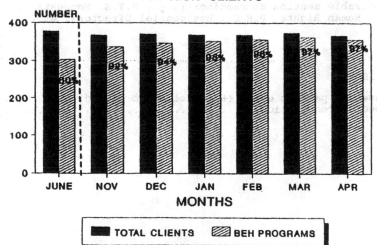

FIGURE 5. Performance Management Program–Feedback and Reinforcer Survey distributed to participants.

Performance Management Program:
Feedback and Reinforcer Survey

Please rate each of the following items for their reinforcement value to you. Score "1" for low value; "2" for moderate value, ad "3" for high value.

Written Recognition and Feedback: Score

1. Letters/notes of appreciation, acknowledgement to
      you individually................................____
      Copy to Division Director, Asst. Director, Director...____
      Copy in personnel file.........................____
2. Certificates, plaques, trophies for achievements.......____
3. Posted compliments, descriptions of accomplishments
      (e.g., on designated bulletin boards).............____
4. Published acknowledgements (e.g., S.T.S. Today; DMR
      Newsletter, state newsletters)....................____
5.   ____
6.   ____
7.   ____

Social Reinforcers:

1. Positive verbal feedback/ praise for performance........____
2. Constructive suggestions/ guidance.....................____
3. Consultation to assist in pursuit of project...........____
4. Meeting with director/ Other for feedback..............____
5. Access to someone to hear your observations and
      recommendations...................................____
6. Support/ recognition from visiting dignitary
      (e.g. Commissioner)...............................____
7. Honorable mention at meetings (e.g., S.T.S. Foundation,
      Human Rights, P.R.C., Residential Directors, etc.)...____
8.   ____
9.   ____
10.   ____

Privileges:

1. Reserved parking space (For designated period)...........____
2. Special recognition......................................____
3.   ____
4.   ____
5.   ____

FIGURE 5 (continued)

Special Activities

1. Invitation to Central Office function/ activity.......... _____
2. Field trip/ site visit to relevant program.............. _____
3. _____
4. _____
5. _____

Tangible Rewards:

1. Small office niceties (possibly available)
   a. Calendars.. _____
   b. Desk blotters................................... _____
   c. Posters... _____
   d. Notebooks....................................... _____
   e. Paperweights.................................... _____
   f. Rugs.. _____
   g. Desk top accessories............................ _____
   h. _____
   i. _____
   j. _____

2. Small personal items
   a. _____
   b. _____
   c. _____
   d. _____

3. Financial support to present research at conference
   (e.g., poster session)............................. _____
4. _____
5. _____
6. _____

resented, for the reasons identified above, are pay for performance, management incentive plans and other types of cash inducements, although some especially enterprising private human service agencies are beginning to avail themselves of those contingencies. In one organization known to us, documented improvements in mutually specified performances are rewarded with cash bonuses.

By recognizing the type of organization in which one is to operate, performance managers should be better able to start positing which contingencies might be most readily capable of being deployed. Nevertheless, only a careful analysis of the contingency network extant in the particular organization of concern can help reveal ongoing and potential sources of reinforcement. Creative practitioners in human service settings will root out and experimentally analyze the function of these elements, thereby improving the quality of services delivered to clients.

REFERENCES

Agnew, J. L., & Redmon, W. K. (1992). Contingency Specifying Stimuli: The Role of "Rules" in Organizational Behavior Management. *Journal of Organizational Behavior Management, 12* (2).

Babcock, R., Sulzer-Azaroff, B., & Sanderson, M. (1989). Increasing staff use of HIV-related infection precautions in a head injury treatment center. Paper presented at the 15th annual meeting of the Association for Behavior Analysis.

Balcazar, F. E., Hopkins, B. L., & Suarez, Y. (1985/86). A critical objective review of performance feedback. *Journal of Organizational Behavior Management, 7,* 65-89.

Balcazar, F. E., Shupert, M. K., Daniels, A. C., Mawhinney, T. C. & Hopkins, B. L. (1989). An objective review and analysis of ten years of publication in the *Journal of Organizational Behavior Management, Journal of Organizational Behavior Management, 10,* 7-37.

Crowell, C. R., Anderson, D. C., Abel, D. M., & Sergio, J. P., (1988). Task clarification, performance feedback, and social praise: Procedures for improving the customer service of bank tellers. *Journal of Applied Behavior Analysis, 21,* 65-71.

Fleming R. K. & Sulzer-Azaroff, B. (1991). Reciprocal peer management: Increasing and maintaining beneficial staff-client interactions. Manuscript submitted for publication.

Fox, C. J. & Sulzer-Azaroff, B., (1989). Effectiveness of supervisor vs. non-supervisor delivered feedback in managing paraprofessional staff. *Journal of Organizational Behavior Management, 2,* 19-35.

Frederiksen, L. W., Riley, A. W., & Myers, J. B. (1984). Matching technology and organizational structure: A case study in white collar productivity improvement. *Journal of Organizational Behavior Management, 6,* 59-80.

George, J. T. & Hopkins, B. L. (1989). Multiple effects of performance contingent pay for waitpersons. *Journal of Applied Behavior Analysis, 22,* 131-141.

Handlin, H. C. (1992). The company built upon the golden rule: Lincoln Electric. In B. L. Hopkins & T. C. Mawhinney (Eds.) *Pay for performance: History, controversy, and evidence.* New York: The Haworth Press, Inc.

Kissel, R. C., Whitman, T. L., & Reid, D. H. (1983). An institutional staff training and self management program for developing multiple self-care skills in severely/profoundly retarded individuals. *Journal of Applied Behavior Analysis, 16,* 395-415.

Komaki, J., Blood, M. R., & Holder, D. (1980). Fostering friendliness in a fast food franchise. *Journal of Organizational Behavior Management, 2,* 151-164.

Journal of Organization Behavior Management, (1986), *Job stress: From theory to suggestion, 8,* 2.

Krapfl, J. E., & Gasparotto, G. (1982). Behavioral systems analysis. In L. W. Frederiksen (Ed.) *Organizational behavior management.* New York: John Wiley & Sons (pp. 21-38).

Luthans, F., Paul, R. & Taylor, L. (1985). The impact of contingent reinforcement on retail salespersons' performance behaviors: A replicated field experiment. *Journal of Organizational Behavior Management, 7*, 2, 25-35.

Malott, R. W. (1992). A theory of rule governed behavior and organizational behavior management. *Journal of Organizational Behavior Management, 12* (2).

Malott, R. W., Shimamune, S., & Malott, M. E. (1992). Rule-governed behavior and organizational behavior management: An analysis of the literature. *Journal of Organizational Behavior Management, 12* (2).

Mawhinney, T. C. (1992). Evolution of Organizational Cultures as Selection by Consequences: The Gaia Hypothesis, Metacontingencies, and Organizational Ecology, *Journal of Organizational Behavior Management, 12* (2).

Mawhinney, T.C. (1986). OBM, SPC, and Theory D: A Brief Introduction, *Journal of Organizational Behavior Management, 8* (1), 89-105.

Mawhinney, T. C. (1979). Intrinsic X extrinsic work motivation: Perspectives from behaviorism. *Organizational Behavior and Human Performance, 24*, 411-440.

Mawhinney, T. C. & Ford, J. D. (1977). The Path-Goal Theory of Leader Effectiveness: An Operant Interpretation. *Academy of Management Review Journal, 2*, 398-411.

Mawhinney, T. C., & Gowen, C. R., III. (1990). Gainsharing and the law of effect as the matching law: A theoretical framework. *Journal of Organizational Behavior Management, 11*, 61-75.

Notz, W. W., Boschman, I. & Tax, S. S. (1987). Reinforcing punishing and extinguishing reward: On the folly of OBM without SPC. *Journal of Organizational Behavior Management, 9*, 33-46.

Stokes, T. F., & Baer, D. M. (1977). An implicit technology of generalization. *Journal of Applied Behavior Analysis, 10*, 349-367.

Sulzer-Azaroff, B., Fox, C. J., Moss, S. M., & Davis, J. M. (1987). Social support and safety on the job. Unpublished paper.

Sulzer-Azaroff, B., Loafman, B., Merante, R. J. & Hlavacek, A. C. (1990). Improving occupational safety in a large industrial plant. *Journal of Organizational Behavior Management, 11*, 99-120.

Zemke, R. E., & Gunkler, J. W. (1982). Organization-wide intervention. In L. W. Frederiksen (Ed.). *Handbook of organizational behavior management* (pp. 565-583). New York: Wiley.